• Bartholomew •

WALK THE
NORTH YORK MOORS

by Brian Spencer

Bartholomew
An Imprint of HarperCollins*Publ*

A Bartholomew Walk Guide
Published by Bartholomew
An Imprint of HarperCollins*Publishers*
77-85 Fulham Palace Road
London W6 8JB

First published 1986
Revised 1989, 1991, 1995

Text © Brian Spencer 1995
Maps © Bartholomew 1995

Printed in Great Britain by
The Edinburgh Press Ltd

ISBN 0 7028 2940 4

86/4/45

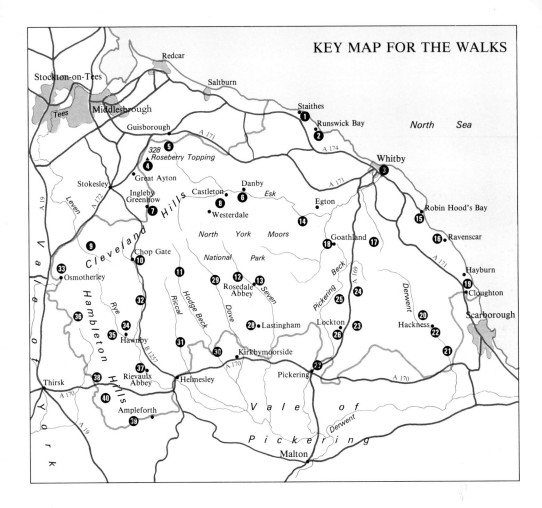

KEY MAP FOR THE WALKS

Redcar

Stockton-on-Tees

Saltburn

Tees

Middlesbrough

Staithes
1

Runswick Bay
2

North   Sea

Guisborough
A 171

A 174

328
Roseberry Topping
5
4

Whitby
3

Great Ayton

Stokesley

A 172

Ingleby
Greenhow
7

Castleton
8

Danby
6

Esk

Egton

A 171

Robin Hood's Bay
15

Westerdale

14

A 19

Leven

Cleveland   *Hills*

North   York   Moors

Goathland
18
17

16 Ravenscar

9

Chop Gate
10

National   *Park*

Pickering   *Beck*

A 169

Hayburn
19
Cloughton

33
Osmotherley

Hambleton   *Hills*

11

29

Rosedale
Abbey
12
13

Seven

Dove

24

Derwent

Scarborough

36

Rye

32

Riccal

Hodge Beck

25

20
Hackness
22

34

35
Hawnby

28 Lastingham

Lockton
26
23

21

37
31

30

Kirkbymoorside

27

Thirsk

38
Rievaulx
Abbey

Helmesley

A 170

Pickering

A 170

40

Vale   *of*

A 19

Ampleforth
39

Derwent

Pickering

Malton

Vale   *of*   *York*

KEY TO SCALE AND MAP SYMBOLS

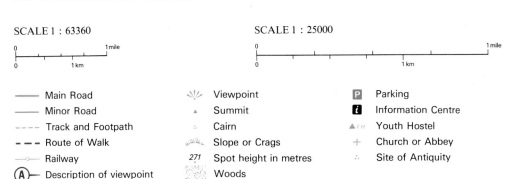

SCALE 1 : 63360

0 — 1 mile
0 — 1 km

SCALE 1 : 25000

0 — 1 mile
0 — 1 km

——— Main Road
——— Minor Road
- - - Track and Footpath
- - - Route of Walk
········ Railway
(A)— Description of viewpoint

🔆 Viewpoint
▲ Summit
⌂ Cairn
� Slope or Crags
271 Spot height in metres
🌳 Woods

P Parking
𝑖 Information Centre
▲ᵥʜ Youth Hostel
+ Church or Abbey
∴ Site of Antiquity

4

1 WALKING FOR ENJOYMENT

Walking is a sport which can fulfil the needs of everyone. It adapts to accommodate all and is the healthiest of all activities. Our inclination might be to walk two or three miles along a gentle track, instead of one of the more arduous long distance routes, but whatever the standard, it will improve general well-being. Walking should be anything from an indivdual affair to a family strolling together, or maybe a group of friends enjoying the fresh air and open spaces of our countryside. There is no need for it to be competitive, or done simply as a means of covering a given distance in the shortest possible time.

As with all other outdoor activities, walking is safe providing a few simple commonsense rules are followed:

a) Make sure you are fit enough to complete the walk.

b) Always try to let others know where you intend going.

c) Be adequately clothed for the weather and always wear suitable footwear.

d) Always allow plenty of time for the walk, especially if it is longer or harder than you have done before.

e) No matter what distance you plan to walk, always allow plenty of daylight unless you are absolutely certain of the route

f) If mist or bad weather comes on unexpectedly, do not panic, but try to remember the last certain feature which you have passed (road, farm, wood, etc) and work out your route from that point on the map.

g) In planning a beach walk, check tide times and make sure you can get off the beach with the tide going out, never wait until it is coming in. Remember there are very few access points through the cliffs on this coast.

h) Long sections of the coastal cliffs are unstable so take care when walking beneath them.

i) Unfotunately accidents can happen even on the easiest of walks. If this should be the case and you need the help of others, make sure that the injured person is safe (i.e. away from falling rocks or the incoming tide). Dial 999 and ask for assistance. This will vary depending on where the accident occured. If it was on the beach or a coastal cliff, ask for the Coastguard Service. Unless the accident has happened within easy access of a road, then it is the responsibility of the Police to arrange evacuation. Always give accurate directions of how to find the casualty and if possible, an indication of the injuries involved.

j) When walking in open country learn to walk with half your vision on the immediate foreground and the other half admiring the scenery, or planning the route ahead. This may sound difficult, especially to a beginner, but once you can adapt to this method your enjoyment will increase.

k) Try to walk at a steady pace, always on the flat of the feet as this is less tiring. Never walk directly up or downhill, but try to find a zig-zag route; never run downhill as you may find yourself out of control. Runninng downhill is also a major cause of erosion on popular hillsides.

l) When walking along a country road, walk on the right and face the traffic. The exception to this rule is, when approaching a blind bend, the walker should cross over to the left and so have a clear view and also be seen in both directions.

m) Finally, always park your car where it will not cause inconvenience to other road users or prevent a farmer from gaining access to his fields. Make sure that you lock the car and hide any valuables before leaving (or preferably, carry all valuables with you).

2 EQUIPMENT

Equipment, and this means clothing, footwear and rucksacks, is essentially a personal thing and depends on several factors, i.e. the type of activity planned, the time of year and weather likely to be encountered.

All too often a novice walker wil spend pounds on a fashionable jacket, but will skimp when it comes to buying footwear or a comfortable rucksack. Blistered and tired feet quickly remove all enjoyment from even the most exciting walk and a poorly balanced rucksack will soon feel as though it is carrying half a hundredweight. Well designed equipment is not only more comfortable, but being better made is longer lasting.

Clothing should be adequate for the day, in other words it should protect the wearer from the elements. In summer a lightweight shirt with sleeves and a decent collar, with the help of a brimmed hat, will keep the sun off. A skirt or slacks or even shorts if your knees are tuned to the sun, together with light woollen socks and lightweight boots or strong shoes, are sufficient for warm weather. A spare pullover and waterproofs carried in the rucksack should, however, be there in case of need.

Winter wear is a much more serious affair, remember that once the body starts to lose heat it becomes much less efficient. Jeans are particularly unsuitable for winter wear and can sometimes be downright dangerous.

With the foregoing 'do's and don'ts' of equipment what should the walker buy? The following guidelines are offered as a suggestion of the most comfortable and economic equipment for enjoyable walking:-

Footwear Several manufacturers market a range of lightweight boots which are moulded to the shape of the feet. These are ideal as they require little or no breaking-in and are suitable for all year round walking. If boots do not appeal, and there are many who cannot wear even the lightest boots, then make sure that the shoes you buy have a good moulded sole and are firm around the lower ankle.

Socks The saying 'there's no substitute for wool' applies to socks more than to any other garment. Woollen socks, thick in winter and lighter for summer, are far more comfortable than any other fibre. Never wear nylon unless you want blistered feet.

Trousers or Skirt Slacks are ideal for walking and breeches even better as they don't catch on twigs, etc. If ladies prefer to walk in skirts, make sure they are flared and do not hobble. Shorts are in order for summer wear, provided the wearer has become used to the sun.

Shirts and Pullover In summer a lightweight cotton shirt or blouse is quite adequate provided it has long sleeves and a collar to keep the sun off. Winter wear should be much warmer and two lightweight woollen pullovers, one at least with a crew neck, are better than one of heavy material.

Jacket Make sure that it is windproof and loose enough to allow for an extra layer of warmer clothing underneath. A hood is essential as it helps keep the cold from blowing down the back of the neck.

Hat In summer wear something to keep the sun off the top of your head and the back of your neck - both vulnerable points. A woollen hat which can be pulled well down is essential for winter as something like 25 per cent of body heat can be lost via an uncovered head. Gloves and a scarf are other winter essentials.

Waterproof Clothing Again this is an area where it pays to buy the best one you can afford. Make sure that the jacket is loose-fitting, has a generous hood and comes down at least to knee level. Waterproof overtrousers will not only complete the protection in rain, but are also windproof. There are many makes on the market and the final choice is obviously personal, but do not be misled by flimsy nylon 'showerproof' affairs and on the other hand remember that garments made from rubberised or plastic material are not only heavy to carry and wear, but trap body condensation.

Rucksack When buying a rucksack bear in mind what you will want to carry inside, as this will give a guide to its size. Modern sacks mould themselves to the contours of the wearer's back and should carry the load fairly high. Wide padded carrying straps ensure comfort and prevent them digging into the wearer's shoulders.

A piece of semi-rigid *plastic foam* carried in the rucksack makes a handy and yet almost weightless seat for open air picnics.

The *area map,* as well as this guide, are essential not only for accurate navigation, but add to the enjoyment of a walk.

Finally a small *first aid kit* is an invaluable help in coping with cuts and other small injuries.

3 PUBLIC RIGHTS OF WAY

Even though most of the area covered by this guide comes within the authority of the North York Moors National Park, it does not mean that there is complete freedom of access to walk anywhere. The bulk of the land within the park is privately owned and what might appear to be an ideal spot for a picnic, or somewhere to excercise the dog, is usually part of another person's livelihood.

In 1949 the National Parks and Access to the Countryside Act tidied up the law covering rights of way. Following public consultation, often as local as Parish Councils, maps were drawn up by the County Authorities of England and Wales to show all the rights of way. Copies of these maps are available for public inspection and are invaluable when deciding controversial sections of little used footpaths. Once on the map, rights of way are irrefutable.

Rights of way mean that anyone may walk freely on a defined footpath, or ride a horse or pedal cycle along a public bridleway. No-one may interfere with this right and the walker is within his rights if he removes any obstruction along the route, providing however, that he has not gone purposely with the intention of removing that obstruction. All obstructions should be reported to the local Highways Authority. Free access to footpaths and bridleways does mean that certain guidelines must be followed. For example, only sit down to rest or picnic where it does not interfere with other walkers or the landowner. All gates must be closed to prevent stock from straying and dogs must be kept under close control – usually interpreted as being on a leash. Motor vehicles must not be driven along a public footpath or bridleway without the landowner's consent. A farmer can put a mature beef bull with a herd of cows or heifers, in a field crossed by a public footpath. Beef bulls such as Herefords (usually brown/red colour) are mostly docile, but dairy bulls like the black and white Friesian are dangerous by nature. It is, therefore, illegal for a farmer to let a dairy bull roam loose in a field open to public access.

All public rights of way within the North York Moors National Park, and used for this guide, have been clearly defined and are marked as such on available maps. They are marked on the Ordnance Survey one inch (1 : 63360) and metric (1 : 50000) maps as red dots for footpaths and red dashes for bridleways. On the OS 1 : 25000 scale the dots and dashes are green. (Red dots and dashes on the 1 : 25000 Outdoor Leisure Maps indicate permitted footpaths and bridleways respectively.)

4 THE MOORS MESSAGE

Fire – uncontrolled fires can devastate miles of moorland which may never fully recover. Don't start fires or drop cigarettes or matches.

Litter – is dangerous as well as unsightly – take it home.

Tread gently – despite surviving all sorts of weather, the moors, their plants and animals are fragile and sensitive.

Fences and walls – keep some animals in and some out, use stiles and gates (and shut them).

Safety – weather conditions can change quickly, are you fully equipped?

Footpaths – are for feet. Bicycles may be ridden on bridleways. Motorcycles and other vehicles should stick to roads.

Dogs – keep dogs on leads at all times. A loose dog running over the moors can be catastrophic for nesting birds, sheep and sometimes the dog itself!

Noise – moorlands should be quiet places, try to keep it that way.

4a A COASTAL CODE

* Enjoy the coast and respect its wildlife.
* Keep your dog under control.
* Take care when walking along clifftops.
* Stay away from the bottom of cliffs – rockfalls are common.
* Be sure not to get cut off by the tide.
* Watch your step – rocks and seaweed can be slippery.
* Observe plants and animals in their own homes – not in yours.
* Always replace overturned rocks.
* Leave the beach as you find it for others to enjoy.

Please note: *Tide tables are available from coastal Information Centres.*

5 MAP READING

Some people find map reading so easy that they can open a map and immediately relate it to the area of countryside in which they are standing. To others a map is as unintelligible as ancient Greek! A map is an accurate but flat picture of the three dimensional features of the countryside. Features such as roads, streams, woodlands and buildings are relatively easy to identify either from their shape or position. Heights on the other hand can be difficult to interpret from the single dimension of a map. The one inch (1 : 63360) maps indicate every 50 foot contour line, whilst the metricated 1 : 25000 and 1 : 50000 maps give the contours at 10 metre intervals. Summits and spot heights are also shown.

The best way to estimate the angle of a slope as shown on any map is to remember that if the contour lines come close together then the slope is steep, the closer the steeper.

Learn the symbols of features shown on the map and when starting out on a walk, line up the map with one or more recognisable feature, both from the map and on the ground; in this way the map will be correctly positioned relative to the terrain. If you know your exact position it should be a simple matter to draw imaginary lines on the map and your position will be where they cross. It should only be necessary to look from the map towards the footpath or objective of your walk and then make for it! This process is also useful for determining your position at any time during the walk.

Taking the skill of map reading one stage further: assuming that there are no easily recognised features nearby, there may be the odd clump of trees and a building or two, but none of them can be related to the map. This is a frequent occurence, but there is a simple answer to the problem and it is where the use of a compass comes in. Simply place the map on the ground, or other flat surface with the compass held gently above the map. Turn the map until the edge is parallel to the   line of the compass needle, which should also point to the top of the map. Lay the compass on the map and adjust the position of both, making sure that the compass needle still points to the top of the map and is parallel to the edge. By this method the map is orientated in a north-south alignment. To find your position on the map, look out for prominent features and draw imaginary lines from them down on to the map. Your position is where these lines cross.

This method of map reading takes a little practice before you can become proficient, but it is worth the effort.

It is all too easy for members of a group of walkers to leave map reading to the skilled member or members of the party. No one is perfect and even the best map reader can make mistakes. Other members of the group should take the trouble to follow the route on the map, so that any errors are spotted before they become problems.

Once you become proficient at map reading, the ultimate is in learning to estimate the length of time required for a walk. First of all find out how long it takes your family or party to walk say, two miles (3 kms) on the flat. Let us asssume the time taken is about one hour and the proposed walk is four miles (6 kms) in length. The next thing you will need to know is how much climbing is involved. From the map let us again assume you will need to climb 200 feet (61 m) in order to reach your objective. Climbing uphill is slower than walking on the level and it usually takes an extra five minutes for each 100 feet (30.5m) of easy climbing. In this case the climb is 200 feet (61 m) and will, therefore, take an extra ten minutes.

To calculate how long it will take for your group to climb 200 feet in 4 miles, use the following formula ;.

4 miles (6km) @	
2 miles per hour	= 2 hour
200 ft (61m) of climbing @	
100 ft (30.5m) per 5 minutes	= 10 minutes
Total time for the walk	= 2 hours 10 mins

Of course, time in this case is purely the walking time and does not allow for breaks or picnics, etc.

6 THE NORTH YORK MOORS NATIONAL PARK

In many other countries, National Parks are wilderness areas, where few people unconnected with running the park live permanently. Countries such as the United States of America have even gone to the length of moving residents off land designated as a National Park. In England and Wales, National Parks are areas of outstanding natural beauty where people still live and work. One of the major functions of a National Park is to preserve, by careful planning control, the landscape and people's livelihoods within its boundary. The National Parks and Access to the Country Act of 1949 led to the formation of the nine National Parks in England and Wales. The North York Moors National Park was designated in 1952.

The word 'National' in the title often leads to misunderstanding. National Parks are not nationalised or in any way owned by the Government. Most of the land within the park is in the private ownership of people who live and work there, be they farmers, private landowners or quarry owners. Certain areas of scenic beauty and ancient buildings around the North York Moors are owned by The National Trust, but these were left as gifts by far-sighted owners as a means of ensuring their preservation.

The North York Moors National Park extends over 553 square miles (1432 sq.km) and is a roughly kidney-shaped area of heather moor and secluded valleys, ending in the east with the dramatic sea cliffs of the Yorkshire coast. The A170 forms the approximate line of the southern boundary and the escarpments of the Hambleton and Cleveland Hills complete the western and northern boundaries.

Administration of the park is controlled by a committee, composed of representatives of North Yorkshire and Cleveland County Councils, four District Councils and also members appointed by the Secretary of State for the Environment.

One of the statutory functions of a Park Authority is the appointment of full-time and voluntary Park Rangers. These are people with particular knowledge of some aspects of the local environment, who are available to give help and advice to visitors. Other functions of the Ranger Service cover assistance to local farmers in such matters as rebuilding damaged walls to prevent stock from straying, or perhaps leading guided walks from one of the Information Centres or the National Park Centre at Danby Lodge.

Danby Lodge is a former shooting Lodge in the Esk Valley set in thirteen acres of formal gardens, woodland and riverside meadow. It provides visitors with an interpretative exhibition of the local environment, film shows and talks, and also offers light refreshments. Permanent Information Centres are based at Sutton Bank and Pickering Railway Station, at the southern terminus of the North York Moors Railway. Temporary Information Caravans are available at popular picnic spots and car parks during summer weekends and Bank Holidays.

There are many carefully waymarked trails, with subjects ranging from the Geological Trail at Ravenscar to the Historical Railway Trail at Goathland, as well as trails on Roseberry Topping above Great Ayton, and the May Beck Trail and Forest Walk near Fylingdales. The imaginative linking of old tracks and pack-horse ways throughout Esk Dale provides walks of varying lengths. Details of these trails and walks are provided on leaflets, issued by the North York Moors National Park, and are usually available from Information Centres.

The North York Moors Association is a voluntary society which arranges guided walks, talks, visits and other activities to help understanding of the North York Moors. For details of membership and programme, see 'The Visitor', the annual newspaper of the North York Moors National Park, and also local press.

7 THE HISTORY OF THE MOORS

Man has lived amid these heather moors since prehistoric times. He erected enigmatic stones and cairns still standing on lonely and windswept heights. On the moor above Commondale village he indulged in a feat of civil engineering requiring thousands of man-hours to build. With nothing more than hand-wielded antler picks he built the two-miles-long rampart of Park Pale. With the coming of Christianity, wayside crosses were erected to guide converts physically as well as spiritually. One of these, Ralph's Cross which stands on a lonely roadside sentinel on Rosedale Head, has been adopted as the symbol for the North York Moors National Park.

When the Romans came into the area, they built a road to the coast which also reached valuable ironstone deposits beyond Wheeldale. They made an early warning system against seaborne attack with a series of signal stations along the coast. Instructors brought recruits from the garrison of York to a training area on Cawthorne Moor and taught them the skills of military camp construction, even finding time for a few experimental designs.

Monastic orders found tranquillity and prosperity side by side. St Aeldred, the third Abbot of Rievaulx, spoke so eloquently when he said: 'Everywhere peace, everywhere serenity and a marvellous freedom from the tumult of the world'.

Most of the religious houses were built in sheltered valleys, but St Hilda chose the wild cliff tops above Whitby. Poor inarticulate monk Caedmon, thought to be only fit to tend the animals, had a wonderous dream here one night and awakening, wrote his *Song of Creation,* the earliest known sacred song in English Literature.

The coast was for ever under attack by seaborne raiders; invaders who came, land hungry, from the north east eventually settled as respectable farmers further inland.

Following the invasion of England in 1066 William the Conqueror and the subsequent guerilla activity of the English, vast areas of countryside were laid to waste. For a time the North York Moors was almost uninhabited and the castles of Helmsley, Pickering and Scarborough were built to control a conquered land. So few people lived here in the Middle Ages that the moors were used as a royal hunting forest. Favoured religious orders settled or expanded their control of men's souls and the riches of both the land and sea.

Henry VIII, in his quarrel with the church, stripped abbeys of their wealth and power, turning out the monks and leaving their magnificent buildings to the ravages of the elements. Unwittingly this quarrel led to a new industry which flourished on the coast for several centuries. This was the working of alum which occurs between Ravenscar and Guisborough. Used to fix the popular Turkey Red dyes, alum was a papal monopoly until broken by the king.

Catherine Parr, Henry VIII's sixth wife, lived for a time at Danby Castle. Most of the castles in this area were held for the Crown during the Civil War. In the manner of warfare of that time, they were starved into submission before surrendering to Cromwell's troops under locally born Sir Thomas Fairfax.

The movement of goods and salt to the coast, preserved fish inland, and wool and produce to other markets, needed trackways and a complex network of ways developed. Many fine examples of flagged packhorse ways can still be seen in Esk Dale and are now linked by a series of waymarked trails. Railways came early with George Stephenson building his line from Whitby through difficult Newton Dale. Later the Victorian entrepreneur George Hudson, an early exponent of cut-price travel, brought the mill workers of the West Riding by rail to the burgeoning coastal resorts of Scarborough and Bridlington.

Farming patterns have changed over the centuries. The tiny subsistencies which followed the breakup of huge monastic sheepwalks and granges have disappeared and large holdings now encroach on the moors. Plantations of 'foreign' pines have replaced natural woodland cut down as fuel for treating ironstone or alum.

Of all the people who have lived around the moors, Captain Cook is the best known. He gravitated towards the coast fom his birthplace in Marton and was fortunate in having far-sighted men for his early employers. They encouraged him to study the art of navigation and set him on a course which was eventually to end with his discoveries in the South Pacific.

This coast has always looked to the east against attack and history repeats itself in the 20th century, with the strange golfball shapes of the Radomes on Fylingdales Moor.

8 GEOLOGY

Geology is partly about the changes which occur to the landscape. The most easily recognisable changes are when huge chunks of cliff drop into the sea after a storm, but where else has change taken place?

Take a look out of the carriage window on a ride through Newton Dale on the North York Moors Railway. The steep-sided gorge would appear to have been carved by a deep and fast flowing river, but look at the river. Pickering Beck is quite a gentle stream, in summer often a mere trickle. Surely this has not carved out the dale? The answer is that the present river has had little effect on the shape of the dale, but a predecessor did. Towards the end of the last Ice Age the North Sea remained frozen while ice thawed. What is now Esk Dale became a deep lake fed by an ever-increasing volume of water unable to find a seaward exit. The lake eventually overflowed with cataclysmic force across Goathland Moor to gouge the ravine of Newton Dale. To its south was Lake Pickering, its bed forming the fertile land of the present-day vale, south of the A170 road.

The River Derwent was diverted about the time of this Ice Age. It originally flowed east into the sea above Scarborough, but now flows south through Forge Valley. As part of a flood prevention scheme, a channel known as the Sea Cut was made along the course of the ancient river in the early part of the 19th century.

Distinctive steep hills such as Roseberry Topping and Cringle Moor, on the north-west escarpment of the moors, were left partially free of the ice sheet; their present shape formed by the ice flowing around their flanks.

Due to earth movements and the shifting of continents, many of the rocks which made these moors, first saw the light of day beneath a prehistoric tropical sea. Ironstone found in Rosedale filtered its way through the waters of a mighty river on some long dead continent. Potash and salt mined at Boulby, 4000 feet beneath the surface, were part of an ancient salt lake. Fossils found beneath Whitby's east cliff, or on the shore of Robin Hood's Bay, swam or crawled in a sea far removed and warmer than our North Sea of today.

To the south west is the White Horse of Kilburn, carved from underlying limestone in 1857 by local schoolmaster John Hodgson and his pupils. Most of the southern edge of the moors is limestone, but to the north the rocks are mostly sedimentary shales left by prehistoric rivers. The coast is a complex of hard and soft stratas easily undermined by the ravages of the sea.

9 WILDLIFE ON THE NORTH YORK MOORS

Of all the wildlife on the moors the red grouse is the most common. Not a truly wild bird, it nevertheless breeds here, living a charmed life, eating the green shoots off young heather until the 'Glorious Twelth'. For four months until 10 December, its chances of survival depend upon its ability to dodge the beaters or be missed by an inaccurate shot.

If the ge'back, ge'back, sound of the grouse is intrusive, then the warbling of the curlews on a fine summer's day is as evocative as any sound can possibly be on these windswept heights. The curlew and its cousins the lapwing and the golden plover may all be seen or heard in the course of a day's walk. Smaller birds such as the skylark and whinchat will also make themselves heard, but possibly not seen, as also will the wheatear. Moorland birds of prey are the merlin, with its low, rapid flight, the hovering kestrel and the hen harrier, which now visits in winter. In the woods and forests, tits, woodpeckers and finches are present.

Numerous colonies of seabirds live around the coastal cliffs. Cormorants, kittiwakes, redshanks and fulmars can be found along with more common species.

Animal life ranges from the rare adder of the heather moors, a much maligned creature which prefers to bask in the sun and will only attack under provocation, to that shy woodland dweller the roe deer. Rabbits and hares are in abundance with the harried fox holding his own in secret places. The other misunderstood creature, the badger, goes on his nocturnal business from setts in the natural woodland.

Never pick up a young hare or fledgling. A mother hare deliberately scatters her offspring over a wide area for safety and knows where they all are. She will probably be frightened off by human scent on a carelessly handled leveret. Young birds are also safe away from the nest as the parents will continue to feed them on the ground.

Plant life depends very much on its environment, heather dominates on the acid moors with bluebells and anemones blooming in the spring in deciduous woodlands. Daffodils, once an endangered species, are now in abundance, not only in famous Farndale, but in quiet pockets throughout the southern dales. On the coast the clayey subsoil of the cliff tops is an ideal place for primroses, and yellow celandines are found in marshy places sheltered from the sea. Hazel and other deciduous trees flourish in deep cuttings close to the sea and even manage to survive away from the effect of salt spray behind some of the high cliffs. Blackthorn and furze are the hardiest shrubs, filling exposed hollows in this zone of high winds and salt spray.

10 LONG DISTANCE WALKS AROUND THE NORTH YORK MOORS

Cleveland Way - 93 miles (150 km)
Many of the walks described in this guide follow parts of the Cleveland Way. This long distance footpath is marked with an acorn symbol. Starting at Helmsley, it follows the western and northern edges of the North York Moors before reaching the sea at Saltburn, then following the coast to Filey Brigg. Accommodation is easily available; bed and breakfast cottages, Youth Hostels and comfortable hotels make it possible to divide the walk into easy stages.
Ebor Way - 70 miles (113 km)

A link between the Yorkshire Dales and the North York Moors. Starts at Ilkley in Wharfedale, crosses the Vale of York by way of the city of York, and joins the Cleveland way at Helmsley. Accommodation can be found in small hotels and guest houses, and also at the Youth Hostels at York and Helmsley.

Reasty to Allerton Forest Walk - 16 miles (26 km)
Waymarked route through Forestry Commission land. Details can be obtained from the Low Dalby Forest Visitor Centre. A distinctive blue anorak badge can be claimed by anyone completing this walk.

Derwent Way - 17 miles (27km) to West Ayton
A series of linked footpaths tracing the route of the river Derwent from its source on Fylingdales Moor as far as West Ayton. The walk continues somewhat artificially through the Vale of Pickering to Malton.

Wolds Way - 76 miles (122 km)
Follows the Yorkshire Wolds as a continuation of the Cleveland Way from Filey to Hessle near Hull. Accommodation can be difficult to find on the sparsely populated Wolds.

Rosedale Circuit - 37 miles (59.5 km)
Starts and finishes in Rosedale Abbey village. Crosses nine dales and involves about 5000 feet (1524 km) of climbing.

The Link - 48 miles (22km)
Waymarked route through the Tabular Hills from Helmsley to Scarborough. Combined with the Cleveland Way it is possible to walk round the perimeter of the North York Moors National Park. Details available from the North York Moors National Park office - (see opposite for address).

USEFUL ADDRESSES :

North York Moors National Park,
The Old Vicarage,
Bondgate,
Helmsley,
York YO6 5BP.   Tel: (01439) 70657

Danby Lodge National Park Centre,
Lodge Lane,
Danby,
Whitby YO21 2NB. Tel: (01287) 660540

★ Pickering Station Information Centre,
    North York Moors Railway,
    Pickering.   Tel: (01751) 73791

★ Sutton Bank Information Centre,
    Sutton,
    Thirsk.   Tel: (01845) 597426

★ National Trust Information Centre,
    Ravenscar.   Tel: (01723) 870138

★ Forest Visitor Centre,
    Low Dalby,
    Pickering.   Tel: (01751) 60295

    ★   Open during summer months only.

Walk 1
STAITHES

3¼ miles (5 km) Easy; muddy on woodland section when wet

Staithes likes to claim Captain Cook as its own, but he was not born in Staithes and neither did he study seamanship here. He was apprenticed to a local draper and the germ of his ambition to become a navigator probably came to the young James Cook as he watched the fishing cobles sail in and out of the harbour which was then open to the ravages of the North Sea.

Houses along the harbour side were frequently wrecked; the cosy Cod and Lobster Inn, the closest remaining building to the harbour, has had to be rebuilt many times.

The design of fishing boats on this exposed coast evolved from the Viking Longships, which came to the north-east coast looking for easy pickings. Known locally as 'cobles', they were broad amidships high in both bow and stern, and able to ride the steep inshore surf.

This walk, after exploring Staithes, follows the coast as far as Port Mulgrave, now almost silted up, but once a busy harbour. It then turns inland to the wooded shelter of Borrowby Dale.

2 Leave the village by the narrow street on the right beyond the Cod and Lobster. Pass the house which claims to be where Cook lived and follow the coast path up the cliff by way of a series of steps. Go past the farm and then out on to open fields.

1 Leave your car at the old railway car park. Walk down the hill into the lower and oldest part of Staithes.

10 Turn right at the road and follow it as far as the main A174. Cross over and turn left into Staithes.

9 Cross the bridge and follow the caravan access lane as far as the road.

8 Turn right at the junction of paths and walk to a gate at the end of the wood. Cross the field and go through a short belt of trees. The track now descends steeply towards a wooden bridge by the caravan site.

7 Cross Dales Beck by a footbridge, follow the path uphill and to the left.

6 Cross the A174 to the slip road then over a step stile. Follow yellow arrows down into the wooded valley.

3 Turn right on a narrow lane away from the sea.

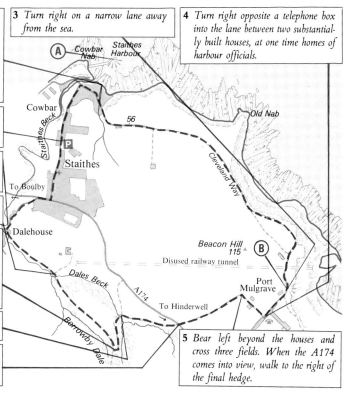

4 Turn right opposite a telephone box into the lane between two substantially built houses, at one time homes of harbour officials.

5 Bear left beyond the houses and cross three fields. When the A174 comes into view, walk to the right of the final hedge.

A Allow plenty of time to explore this quaint fishing village; one of the best vantage points is from the outer harbour wall. Access is by way of the beach beneath Cowbar Nab, so make sure you do not get cut off by the incoming tide.

B Viewpoint of Port Mulgrave where iron-ore was brought along a tunnel on a narrow gauge railway from mines around Boulby.

Walk 2
KETTLENESS AND RUNSWICK BAY
5½ miles (9 km) Moderate

0 ——————————— 1 mile
0 ——————— 1 km

Kettleness, high on the cliff tops, was once a thriving mining village whose menfolk toiled beneath the sea to win ironstone, which was sent to Middlesborough along the coast railway. Mines and railway are now closed and Kettleness is once

again a tiny farm settlement. In 1829 a large portion of the village slid into the sea and even though the present day houses seem to be safe, gradual erosion is slowly threatening them.

Runswick Bay is one of the most

picturesque villages along the coast. More open than Staithes or Robin Hood's Bay, it is protected from north winds and made up of houses scattered across the hillside, each seeming to sit on its own little terrace.

11 *Turn left along the coast path. Go downhill through an area of landslip towards the beach. Follow the row of summer cottages to Runswick Bay.*

12 *Explore Runswick Bay and return by the same route back to 11.*

13 *Bear left at the junction to follow the cliff path back to Kettleness.*

1 *Follow the cliff path to the right away from Kettleness as directed by the Cleveland Way sign.*

Hinderwell

Cleveland Way

Dismantled railway

A174

Runswick Bay

Runswick Bay

Hob Holes

Kettleness Ironstone Mines (disused)

103

Kettle Ness

Kettleness

E

D

C

A

B

Scratch Alley

131

Cleveland Way

Goldsborough

Fox & Hounds Inn

10 *Go through a gap in the hedge, turn right along a clearly-defined path to the railway bridge. Cross the bridge and follow the path downhill.*

9 *Walk to the right of the old windbent hedge.*

8 *Turn left through the gate and follow left side of the fence. Climb the low fence at next field boundary.*

7 *Follow right-hand side of the hedge.*

6 *Go through the gate, turn left and follow the field boundary. There is no path between points 6 and 10; keep close to the field boundaries.*

2 *Turn right then left to climb the embankment and tunnel portal of the old railway and follow the path.*

3 *Turn right away from the coast along a raised cart track.*

4 *Turn right by road through Goldsborough, where there is a comfortable little pub, Fox and Hounds.*

West Barnby

East Barnby

A174

5 *Where the road turns sharply to the right, walk ahead on a wide track hedged on both sides.*

A Views of Kettle Ness, a complex of landslip and jagged sea-washed rocks. Scene of many shipwrecks.

B Note the route of a previous section of the railway.

C Scratch Alley, a Roman Early Warning Station, can be reached by a field path from Goldsborough.

D Humps and hollows in the field on the right mark the site of Kettleness Ironstone Mine.

E Hob Holes, a series of overgrown cliff-side hollows, were supposed to be the home of hobgoblins, but were made by jet miners in Victorian times. Local people once brought their children here to be cured of whooping cough.

Walk 3
WHITBY
2½ miles (4 km) Easy

The long march of history has left its indelible mark on Whitby. The street patterns around the harbour would be recognisable even today to Captain Cook, whose locally built *Endeavour* took him on his voyages.

Whitby reached its zenith as a port in the heyday of whaling and many fine Regency buildings above the west town speak of the wealth created from this barbaric industry.

If you can ignore the candy floss of West Shore and explore the byways of this fascinating town, it will become a journey of discovery where tantalising links with the past are found around almost every corner. On a damp misty day visions of Bram Stoker's Dracula may lurk near the sombre tombstones on top of East Cliff.

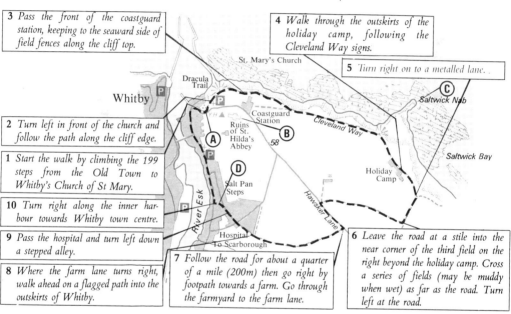

3 *Pass the front of the coastguard station, keeping to the seaward side of field fences along the cliff top.*

4 *Walk through the outskirts of the holiday camp, following the Cleveland Way signs.*

5 *Turn right on to a metalled lane.*

2 *Turn left in front of the church and follow the path along the cliff edge.*

1 *Start the walk by climbing the 199 steps from the Old Town to Whitby's Church of St Mary.*

10 *Turn right along the inner harbour towards Whitby town centre.*

9 *Pass the hospital and turn left down a stepped alley.*

8 *Where the farm lane turns right, walk ahead on a flagged path into the outskirts of Whitby.*

7 *Follow the road for about a quarter of a mile (200m) then go right by footpath towards a farm. Go through the farmyard to the farm lane.*

6 *Leave the road at a stile into the near corner of the third field on the right beyond the holiday camp. Cross a series of fields (may be muddy when wet) as far as the road. Turn left at the road.*

A An intricately carved memorial column at the top of the steps is to Caedmon, a medieval monk from nearby St Hilda's Abbey, whose *Song of Creation* is the earliest known religious poem in English literature. The exterior of St Mary's Church, dating from AD1110, has been modified across the centuries, but its interior is unique. A profusion of panelling and box pews date from the 17th and 18th centuries.

The Chomley family pew with its barley-sugar-twist is interesting.

B St Hilda founded the abbey in AD657. She was the daughter of a King of Northumberland and her abbey, which housed both monks and nuns, grew over the centuries into its present but ruined state. Abandoned after the Dissolution of 1593, it suffered further damage in 1914 during the bombardment of

the town by a German cruiser.

C The view of Saltwick Nab, especially when the sea is rough, is in dramatic contrast to bustling Whitby. Saltwick Nab, a jumble of sedimentary rocks, is National Trust property; free access is by the signposted track to the left below the holiday camp.

D Salt Pan Steps, is one of many old ways out of the town.

15

CAPTAIN COOK'S MONUMENT AND ROSEBERRY TOPPING

5 miles (8 km) Strenuous; steep section 700 feet (213 m)

From the A173 Guisborough to Great Ayton road one cannot help noticing the conical bulk of Roseberry Topping, Cleveland's Matterhorn. More than 1000 feet high, it can claim the accolade of being a mountain and looks grand and precipitous no matter how it is viewed. A relic of the Ice Age, its hoary head protruded as a nunatak from the surrounding ice.

Great Ayton is where Captain Cook went to school; the building although rebuilt in 1785, still stands and has been converted into a Captain Cook Museum. In 1934 a house, said to have been owned by Cook's father and therefore assumed to have direct links with the great navigator, was shipped complete with its creeping ivy, and rebuilt brick by brick by the Australian Government in Melbourne's Fitzroy Gardens. The original site of the house is marked by an obelisk made of stones from

Point Hicks where Cook first made his Australian landfall on 20 April, 1770. According to local authority, Cook's connection with the house was, at most, only slight for his father is not supposed to have bought it until Cook was a grown man and away at sea most of the time! There is even doubt about the authenticity of Cook senior's connection and one suspects that perhaps the Australian Government may have been hoodwinked into an expensive exercise.

What is certain, though, is the 60 foot obelisk on Easby Moor, erected in 1827 by Robert Campion, a Whitby banker. A plaque on the base of the pinnacle tells, in heavy Victorian prose, the story of Cook's epic and brilliant career, which started from fairly humble beginnings at Marton near Middlesbrough and ended in tragedy on a South Sea island beach after a lifetime of discovery.

The Cleveland Way follows the northern escarpment and crosses Easby Moor; this walk uses the route as far as Roseberry Topping. Where it crosses Great Ayton Moor, it goes through an area filled with relics of our prehistoric forebears. To the right of the track, hut circles and other earthworks can easily be seen, especially after a programme of heather burning.

Roseberry Topping, the crux of the walk, is a hard climb no matter how it is approached. There is no dishonour, if when you see it towering above Roseberry Common, you decide to call it a day, and turn left to join the track to Airey Holme Farm. But, if you do want to climb to the top, then whenever possible, avoid the direct approach by using a zig-zag route. The view from the top will be worth all the effort, but remember that the rocky summit has some dangerous drops, so keep away from the edge!

A Captain Cook's Monument. One of the finest viewpoints on the North York Moors; below is the Cleveland Plain with the Pennines stretching as a hazy line from left to right. The bulk of Cross Fell, the Pennines' highest point (2830 feet; 893 m), and the source of Cleveland's main river, the Tees, can be seen to the north west on a clear day. Behind the monument a wild vista of moorland stretches into the distance.

B The proliferation of ancient enclosures, hut circles, cairns and field systems on the moor speaks of habitation in a warmer climate than now.

C Roseberry Topping. All of Cleveland is spread beneath this airy mountain. Until the 17th century it was called 'Osburye Toppyne' and in troubled times warning beacons were lit on its summit. It warned of the approaching Spanish Armada and later Charles Stuart's rebellious Jacobites, but more recently it has only shone out for happy occasions such as the Coronation of Queen Elizabeth II.

Over

7 Leave Newton Moor and go left through a gate at the angle of the wall. Walk downhill on a well-made path towards the col below Roseberry Topping. Climb the hillside using the zig-zag route away from the direct path whenever possible.

8 Walk carefully downhill by a path slanting left below the south side of the summit. Zig-zag towards the lower path and cross a short section of moorland grazing to join the track to Airy Holme Farm.

9 Follow the metalled access lane downhill from the farm as far as the road. Turn right and the railway bridge is about 250 yards (228 m) away, with the platform or car park approached by steps below a wicket gate on the left.

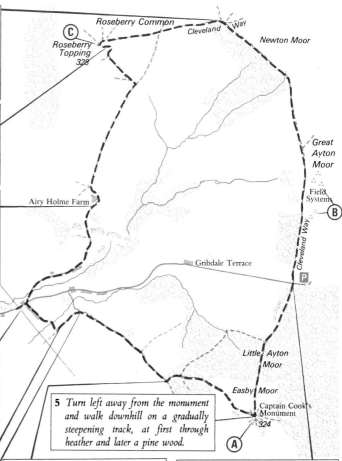

1 The walk starts and finishes at Great Ayton station where there is ample car parking when not travelling by train. Turn right over the railway bridge then almost immediately right again along a short lane past two or three houses and a chicken farm, into a small field.

2 Go left at the junction of cart tracks.

3 Turn right on to a track heading towards the lower moors, at first there are hedges on either side then trees later on.

4 Turn left away from the track, aiming uphill by a path alongside a stone wall to enter the forest at a narrow gate. Turn sharply right beyond the gate and climb steeply uphill along a fire break, crossing a forest track on the way. The path leaves the confines of the pine trees at the top of the rise, to follow a gentler course across the heather moor.

5 Turn left away from the monument and walk downhill on a gradually steepening track, at first through heather and later a pine wood.

6 Cross the metalled forest access road at the car park and climb up to the moor by the stepped path. Follow the Cleveland Way signs upwards to the forest boundary wall at the top of the rise. Keep to the right of the wall and along a wide path of springy turf with heather moor on the right. This is Great Ayton Moor, leading to Newton Moor.

17

HUTTON VILLAGE AND
GUISBOROUGH WOODS

0 ⊢————————————————————— 1 mile
0 ————————————————— 1 km

3 miles (5 km) Easy; one steep downhill section

Guisborough is little more than a dormitory for Middlesbrough, but at least its main shopping area has kept the character of the ancient market street, with cobbled verges fronting attractive shops. The town is built on ancient foundations: there was an important Augustinian Priory here until the Dissolution.

Founded in 1119 by Robert de Brus, the magnificent east end still stands beyond the parish church.

Hutton Village, where the walk starts, is an enclave of commuter homes of Tees-side executives and down the road is Hutton Hall, one-time home of an iron master.

The walk leads easily through Hutton Wood before reaching the contrast of Hutton Moor. Leaving the moor, the path skirts the foot of Highcliff Nab, a partially quarried gritstone outcrop, before returning to Hutton Bridge by way of Highcliff Wood plantation.

8 *Turn right into Hutton Village to return to the starting point.*

Guisborough

Dismantled railway

Hutton Hall

7 *Turn left along the gravel track, moving slightly uphill back into the forest. Follow this track around the spur of the hillside.*

6 *Turn sharp left below the rounded corner of the Nab and walk steeply downhill along a firebreak. (N.B. The path can be slippery when wet.) Ignore side tracks until the wide path above the housing estate is reached, at the forest's lower edge.*

Ⓒ

136

1 *The walk starts along the bridleway to the right of the Hutton Village road, immediately before the first houses. Climb steadily through mixed plantations of mature conifers.*

Hutton Village

319
Highcliff Nab
Highcliff Wood

Guisborough Woods

Ⓑ

2 *Carry on ahead and uphill at the crossing of forest tracks.*

Hutton Wood

Hutton Lowcross Woods

Cleveland Way

5 *Turn left away from the moor. Go through a gate into the forest. Follow yellow arrow markers to the right across two forest rides.*

To Roseberry Topping
2 Km
271
Hutton Moor

Ⓐ

3 *Go through the gate at the upper edge of the forest and out on to the open moor. The Cleveland Way is joined at this point.*

4 *Turn left away from the track at a low-lying rock painted with a yellow waymark arrow. Walk forwards on a narrow path across the heather moor. It is marked by occasional cairns as*

far as the boundary wall. Turn right on reaching the wall and follow it, slightly uphill, still on the moorland path, as far as the corner of the forest at the top of the rise.

A The track was once part of an ecclesiastical route between Rosedale Abbey and Guisborough Priory.

B Look back over the rolling

moorland towards the pinnacle of Captain Cook's Monument on Easby Moor. To the right stretches the Cleveland Plain and industrial Tees-side.

C Highcliff Nab, a natural outcrop of gritstone. Viewpoint for Tees-side with the North Sea on the right.

AINTHORPE AND
DANBY CASTLE   3¼ miles (5 km) Easy

The moors of Ainthorpe Rigg ('rigg' is the local name for a broad ridge and comes from the Old Norse) were populated in prehistoric times by a people who have left us a tantalising glimpse of their technology. Cairns and dykes dot the moor, together with hut circles and field systems, suggesting

that the moors were once more fertile than today.

Catherine Parr, the sixth and only wife to outlive Henry VIII, would have known Danby Castle; her family owned the castle and lands around it in the 16th century. Now a farm, what remains of the

original building speaks of a much grander house. Manorial courts still meet in a room in the oldest part, but only to settle grazing disputes.

Duck Bridge crosses the Esk, no longer carrying trains of packhorses, but still strong enough to bear the weight of an occasional car.

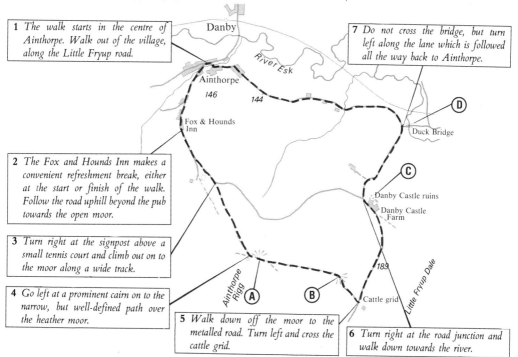

1 *The walk starts in the centre of Ainthorpe. Walk out of the village, along the Little Fryup road.*

2 *The Fox and Hounds Inn makes a convenient refreshment break, either at the start or finish of the walk. Follow the road uphill beyond the pub towards the open moor.*

3 *Turn right at the signpost above a small tennis court and climb out on to the moor along a wide track.*

4 *Go left at a prominent cairn on to the narrow, but well-defined path over the heather moor.*

5 *Walk down off the moor to the metalled road. Turn left and cross the cattle grid.*

6 *Turn right at the road junction and walk down towards the river.*

7 *Do not cross the bridge, but turn left along the lane which is followed all the way back to Ainthorpe.*

Danby · Ainthorpe · River Esk · 146 · 144 · Fox & Hounds Inn · Duck Bridge · **D** · **C** · Danby Castle ruins · Danby Castle Farm · Ainthorpe Rigg · **A** · **B** · 189 · Cattle grid · Little Fryup Dale

A Viewpoint. Esk Dale winds its way through the moors and Roseberry Topping can be seen as the conical hill in the distance.

B Viewpoint. Little Fryup Dale is directly below. To the right of the prominent ridge on its far side is

Fairy Plain, where a friendly hobgoblin once lived.

C Danby Castle. Try to visualise its former size from partly ruined walls beyond the farm house. Manorial courts still meet in the tiny room above the main building. The room

is open to the public by key, which can be obtained from the farmer.

D Duck Bridge. One of the finest examples of a pack-horse bridge in Esk Dale. Cars use this bridge, so take care, as drivers are blind on reaching its sharp crest.

19

INGLEBY INCLINE
7½ miles (12 km) Strenuous; one climb 807 feet (246 m)

The fortunes of Tees-side iron masters were partially founded on the efforts of men who mined in remote places on the high moors. The richest ironstone deposits were above Rosedale to the south of the Cleveland Hills. Getting the ore down to the steep northern escarpment created something of a problem and a way round it was to build a railway around the skyline of Rosedale, visiting all the major mines. Partially processed ore was carried in wagons across the moor to Bolworth Crossing and then straight down the steep side of Greenhow Bank by an incline and so to the furnaces of Middlesbrough. Engines used for hauling the wagons spent all their working lives on the skyline track, unless they needed major repair, when they had to be lowered down the incline. The line was closed in 1928, but there are still people around who will remember riding up the incline in empty wagons.

When you walk down the steep track of the incline, you should be able to find many relics of this unique mode of transport. At the top are the substantial foundations of a winding house and then at the bottom of the incline, close by the point where a forest road joins from the left, is an obvious emergency run off, to stop escaping trucks causing any damage further down the line. Men who worked the track lived in a row of cottages about 500 yards (457 m) beyond this point.

Contrasting with the brute strength of hauling heavy wagons up and down the incline, the well-maintained moorland track above it is a still tangible reminder of gentler transport on what was once a coach road. Travellers from Kirkbymoorside to Stokesley and Guisborough came this way, possibly not enjoying the view as we can, for even on a well-maintained track, the jolting experienced in a mailcoach would soon remove all pleasurable thoughts.

The walk is one of many contrasts. Farmland soon gives way to forest and then a huge vista of heather moor opens up at the top of the steep climb of Ingleby Bank. If blessed with fine weather, then the walk along Greenhow Bank by the coach road is one of the finest possible. The descent of the incline is a link with our industrial past and the final stretch of the walk takes us through lush farmland with a bluebell wood at the finish.

Ingleby Greenhow was mentioned in the Domesday Book, but the region at that time was a wild and inhospitable place, harassed first by the Danes and later by the Normans. The Church of St Stephen was founded sometime in the 12th century, but the building we see today is mainly as it was altered and rebuilt in the 18th century.

A Viewpoint. To the north is the monolith of Captain Cook's Monument on Great Ayton Moor, beyond is Roseberry Topping. Middlesbrough and Tees-side complete the northern horizon and the North Sea can often be glimpsed beyond the towers of the ICI Refinery.

B The route follows the old Kirbymoorside to Stokesley coach road and is marked by roadside standing stones. The old custom of leaving small coins on top of the more prominent stones is carried on even today, a link with ancient sacrifice to the gods who looked after the moorland travellers.

C Viewpoint. The valley below is Ingleby Beck and beyond lies Urra Moor, then Hasty Bank, Cringle and Live Moors, all ancient places dotted with tumuli and prehistoric cairns.

D Viewpoint looking north along the valley of Ingleby Beck.

E This group of buildings housed railwaymen who worked trains up and down the incline.

F Ingleby Greenhow Church. The low building with its squat dovecote-like tower, is typical of many village churches around the moors. Numerous interesting features inside and out make this church, built on ancient foundations, well worth a visit.

Over

0   1 mile

0   1 km

2 Cross the field, away from the tree, keeping slightly left of the belt of trees on the far side.

3 Turn sharp left to follow the field boundary away from Ingleby Manor house.

4 Turn right along a metalled road, walk as far as a group of cottages and a farm house on the edge of the pine forest of Battersby Plantation.

1 The walk starts from Ingleby Greenhow Church. Walk for about 150 yards (137 m) through the village on the Battersby road. Turn right at a footpath sign between two houses. Follow the garden fences into the field near a large and prominent tree.

5 Go through the farm yard and bear left along the forest road. The surface of the road soon deteriorates, but is still an ideal way to climb steep Ingleby Bank.

17 Cross the stream by stepping stones to reach the church.

16 Climb down a short flight of stone steps to the road and turn right.

6 Turn sharp right on a stoney track at the top of Ingleby Bank.

15 Cross a series of fields, using stiles as landmarks when the path is indistinct. Immediately beyond the next farm turn half right, again crossing fences and boundaries by stiles, and walk towards the belt of trees sheltering Ingleby Beck. Turn left along the edge of the wood.

7 The Cleveland Way joins the route at this point and the wide sandy path can be seen stretching far to the south as an almost level track.

14 Turn right along the farm drive and keep to the left of Low Farm. Follow a field path beyond the farm.

13 Go left, then right, around the front of the farmhouse. Follow the farm lane, left, as far as the road and turn right.

12 Cross the stream at a footbridge. Climb the sloping field opposite by the rough path to Wood's Farm.

11 Go left away from the track, through a gate on the far edge of a small wood. Cross two fields leading towards the shallow depression of Ingleby Beck.

8 Look out for a line of shooting butts alongside the track. Turn right and walk through the ruined winding house.

10 At the bottom of the incline, join a rough road and continue ahead on a level cinder track.

9 Turn right into the cutting and walk down the incline.

Map labels: To Great Ayton & Stokesley; Ingleby Greenhow; To Battersby; 128; F; Stepping Stones; Ingleby Manor; 144; Bank Foot; Battersby Crag; Battersby Moor; A; Ingleby Bank; Low Farm; Wood's Farm; Battersby Plantation; 179; Cleveland Way; Ingleby Moor; B; Greenhow Bank; C; E; 198; Ingleby Beck; Winding House ruins; 432; Incline Top; Grouse butts; D; Dismantled railway; Greenhow Moor; Bloworth Crossing

Walk 8
CASTLETON AND WESTERDALE
8 miles (13 km) Moderate / strenuous

In 1089 Robert de Brus, one of William the Conqueror's knights, built the castle which gave Castleton its name. Built not of stone, but as a wooden defensive palisade on top of a man-made earth mound, it was part of the reign of terror during the 'harrying of the north' which followed the Conquest. It was built as a means of subjugating the unruly, part-Viking people, who lived here at the time. The castle served its purpose, but never grew to be another Scarborough and was dismantled in 1216. Castleton is one of those villages where time goes by, no longer part of the frenetic ironstone mining boom of the last century, but still very much the central village for farms in the surrounding valleys.

High heather moorland is crossed by breezy roads constructed along ridges above sheltered valleys which support small, but prosperous, dairy and sheep farms. Sheep spend their summers on the common grazing of the moors, but are usually brought closer to their owners' farms in winter.

Westerdale village has almost a frontier aspect about it, made all the more apparent by the way the moors reach down to the village limits. A former shooting lodge once accommodated Victorian sportsmen who came for a season of grouse shooting on nearby moors. No longer do we hear of the massive bags of bygone years, but grouse are still carefully nurtured amongst the heather, until the fateful 12th of August, when parties and syndicates can enjoy their traditional sport.

Before the coming of roads suitable for wheeled vehicles, commercial traffic in the area relied upon sure-footed pack-horses. Trains of these sturdy beasts would wend their way, either with salted fish from the sea or with wool, to West Riding markets, bringing back supplies of goods essential to life on the remote moors. Flagged ways still run throughout Esk Dale, and several narrow, gracefully-arched bridges mark the route of the ancient pack-horse trails.

A Little remains of Castleton's wooden palisaded 'castle', other than the Motte's earthen mound..

B The holes high up in the gable end of an old barn on the right, close to West Green Farm, were part of a dove cote. The birds were bred as a cheap source of meat from medieval to Victorian times.

C Viewpoint. The high level road across heather-covered Castleton Rigg is made for leisurely motoring. The view from this point takes in a wide sweep of moors: to the south are Danby High Moor and Westerdale Moor, with Ralph's Cross (the symbol of the North York Moors National Park) pointing the way to Rosedale Head. Commondale Moor, with its massive prehistoric earthworks, lies to the north, above Esk Dale.

D Note the restored bee house at the bottom of the kitchen garden. The niches in the stone wall were made to hold straw skeps, an early form of beehive.

E Hunter Stee Pack-Horse Bridge. There are several narrow hump-backed bridges in Esk Dale, designed with high arches for maximum strength; they were built for pack-horse traffic, a more convenient method of moving goods across the wide moors and steep valley sides in the days before roads. A line of flagstones, beyond the bridge and still faintly visible in the grass alongside the hedgerow, marks the line of the old track.

Over

0 _____ 1 mile
0 _____ 1 km

19 Join the main road and walk downhill into Castleton.

18 Cross the road and bear left on to the moorland path, climbing steadily all the time

17 Walk downhill towards the stream and cross by means of the footbridge. Climb up to the road.

16 Follow the track to the left in front of the farmhouse boundary. Turn right through a gate, then left at another to follow a footpath sign to 'Castleton'. Keep close to the wall and aim for the upper edge of a small wood.

1 Park and walk down Castleton's main street, then turn right along the Danby Dale road (Wandels Lane). Cross the stream below Danby Low Moor and climb uphill following the road to the right.

2 Turn right, away from the road on to the drive, then go between the house and the farm buildings. Walk towards a signposted stile on the far side of the field. There is no obvious path but the route ahead is roughly parallel to the narrow brook and a series of gates marks the right of way.

3 The route moves away from the brook to higher ground; continue lining up gates in boundary walls.

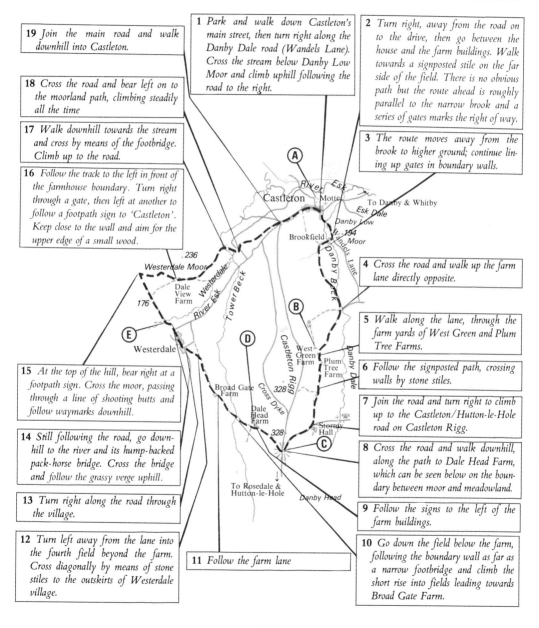

4 Cross the road and walk up the farm lane directly opposite.

5 Walk along the lane, through the farm yards of West Green and Plum Tree Farms.

6 Follow the signposted path, crossing walls by stone stiles.

7 Join the road and turn right to climb up to the Castleton/Hutton-le-Hole road on Castleton Rigg.

8 Cross the road and walk downhill, along the path to Dale Head Farm, which can be seen below on the boundary between moor and meadowland.

9 Follow the signs to the left of the farm buildings.

10 Go down the field below the farm, following the boundary wall as far as a narrow footbridge and climb the short rise into fields leading towards Broad Gate Farm.

15 At the top of the hill, bear right at a footpath sign. Cross the moor, passing through a line of shooting butts and follow waymarks downhill.

14 Still following the road, go downhill to the river and its hump-backed pack-horse bridge. Cross the bridge and follow the grassy verge uphill.

13 Turn right along the road through the village.

12 Turn left away from the lane into the fourth field beyond the farm. Cross diagonally by means of stone stiles to the outskirts of Westerdale village.

11 Follow the farm lane

23

SCUGDALE AND LIVE MOOR

4 miles (6 km) Moderate

0   1 mile

0   1 km

If you had come into Scugdale about a hundred years ago, you would have found a very different state of affairs to this quiet backwater of to-day. For a start there would hardly have been a tree standing; most of the trees seen today have been planted by the Forestry Commis-sion. The biggest impact, however, would have been the number of people round and about, especially on Sundays, when all those engaged in mining were spending their only day above ground. Ironstone min-ing was an intensive industry both on the edge of Whorlton Moor and in pockets along the valley bottom. Near the start of this walk at Huthwaite, lie the spoil heaps of the Marquis of Aislesbury's Scugdale Iron Mine. A light railway from the mine ran across the field beyond the telephone box - you can still see traces of an embankment.

7 Left along the escarpment edge on a clearly-defined path winding its way through heather and past occasional outcropping boulders.

8 Cross the stile and walk down the stepped path between two sections of plantation.

9 Go left at the bottom of the firebreak to join a bridle-way along the forest edge back to Huthwaite Green.

6 Turn left on a path climbing in a sweeping curve round the prominent knoll of Gold Hill.

5 Aim uphill, keeping to the left of the top corner of Snotterdale Plantation. Cross the moorland boundary fence by an easy one-step stile and turn right on a wide sandy track.

4 Go between gate posts in the boundary wall and out on to the open heather moor. Climb gently uphill avoiding the marshy spot which fills a hollow immediately beyond the gate. The worst parts of a swamp are in-variably brightest green, from spagnum moss which grows only in the wettest places.

3 Follow the narrow stream uphill towards the boundary wall between moor and farmland.

2 Turn left away from the road on to the easily rising farm track. Walk towards Fog Close Farm, but do not go as far as the farm buildings. Turn right in front of the farm and climb towards them through a line of ancient hawthorns.

1 Park somewhere convenient to Huth-waite Green; usually space is avail-able by the telephone box. Walk along the Scugdale road as far as the right-hand bend beyond Sparrow Hall.

Map labels: Glider Field, Gold Hill, Cleveland Way, 315, Live Moor, Snotterdale Plantation, To Swainby Huthwaite, 139, Huthwaite Green, Fog Close Farm, Snotterdale, Sparrow Hall, Scugdale Beck, 186. Points: A, B, C, D, E.

A Views of upper Scugdale and Whorlton Moor.

B Viewpoint. Whorlton Moor is to the left, the north-western limit of the Cleveland Hills. Whorlton comes from 'hvirfill', Old Norse for Round Hill.

C Glider Field. Take care not to stray into the path of a landing air-craft.

D Viewpoint. Cleveland and indus-trial Tees-side stretch from the Pen-nines in the west to the North Sea in the east. The prominent conical hill in the middle distance to the north-east is Roseberry Topping.

E The overgrown spoil heaps on either side of the path are from iron-stone mines, once a staple industry of the moors.

CHOP GATE AND SEAVE GREEN

```
0                                1 mile
├────┬────┬────┬────┬────┬────┤
0                          1 km
```

2 miles (3¼ km) Easy; Muddy below Chop Hill when wet

The twin hamlets of Chop Gate and Seave Green find shelter from all but the hardest winter storms. Tucked away in a hollow at the top of Bilsdale, they are completely surrounded by two arms of the Cleveland Hills, with Hasty Bank blocking off the northern access. The sun often manages to smile on this part of the dale even when the weather has closed in all around.

Both villages lie astride the B1257 Helmsley to Stokesley road; beyond Hasty Bank it drops steeply down Clay Bank to Broughton and Stokesley, where the A172 leads to Middlesbrough.

They pronounce Chop Gate, 'Chop Yat' locally; Gate presumably means a way or road or even the gap or 'gate' at the dale head, but the word 'Chop' is a curious one. Having nothing to do with a cut of meat, even in a countryside mostly given over to rearing sheep, 'chop' comes from the Old English 'ceop', meaning pedlar. Pedlars and tinkers were once an essential part of life on the remote moors. Not only did they carry supplies such as cattle remedies and pots and pans, but they could often offer small luxury items like ribbons and buttons to farmers' wives. As well as being a small but important commercial enterprise, they had an essential link with the outside world and were able to carry messages and pass items of news and gossip

9 *Go left away from the road, through a gate at the near corner of the third field beyond the main road. Follow the boundary hedge down the gently sloping field. Turn left at the bottom and cross a fence stile.*

10 *Keep to the right of field boundaries as far as an old gate. Go through it, keeping to the left of the hedge and follow this as far as the main road and stile into car park.*

1 *Leave your car in Chop Gate picnic area. Turn half right from the car park and walk over the road to a farm drive opposite. Climb the fence stile on the right of the drive. There is no obvious path at this point, but the right of way takes a diagonal course over the field to join the farm lane at a gate in the top wall.*

2 *Turn left, follow track up to farm.*

8 *Turn sharp right between a group of cottages on to the Raisdale road and away from the main road. N.B. There is an inn a little way down the main road, which would make a suitable diversion for refreshment.*

3 *Following signs, go to the right around the back of the farm house to join a cart track.*

7 *Turn left into the walled moorland access lane down Chop Hill. Follow it as far as the road at Chop Gate. N.B. The lower portion of the lane is sunken and can be muddy.*

6 *Keep right of a large barn and cross the field along a faint path.*

5 *Cross the road by the last houses in Seave Green and walk up the lane.*

4 *Go left through the farmyard and right on to a farm access lane. Walk downhill through the little valley and, lower down, along the stream bank.*

Map labels: To Stokesley; Seave Green; Cold Moor Lane; B; 176; Chop Hill; B1257; Bilsdale Beck; Raisdale Road; Chop Gate; Inn; A; William Beck Farm; P; Raisdale Beck; 157; To Helmsley

A Viewpoint. The Cleveland Hills, dominated by the 1200 foot (366 m) Bilsdale West Moor television transmitter, fill the far horizon. Closer to hand, Bilsdale itself runs from right to left as the main valley. Bisecting it a little to the left is Raisdale where a moorland road climbs over Cringle Moor. The road drops steeply down Carlton Bank past the Three Lords' Stone where three estates once met.

B Viewpoint. Look back in the direction from which you have just come. Left to right are the rolling masses of Urra, Slape Wath and Bilsdale East Moors separating Bilsdale from remote Bransdale.

BRANSDALE
5 miles (8 km) Moderate / strenuous

Bransdale is about as remote as you can get into the depths of the North York Moors. Reached by a narrow unfenced road from Kirkbymoorside and Gillamoor, or an even lonelier one north from Helmsley, the dale shelters beneath the arms of Rudland Rigg and Bilsdale Moor. Forested slopes of Bransdale Moor to the north link the moorland arms to protect this south-facing hollow. Despite its altitude and remoteness, Bransdale manages to smile on the visitor who takes the trouble to explore this Shangri-la of the moors.

Hodge Hob used to live on the moors above this dale when people were not so sophisticated as they are today. A friendly little chap, he would help in the kitchen or do odd jobs around the farm at night, if the farmer or his wife were kind enough to leave him a spot of bread and milk, but woe betide anyone who crossed him, because all kinds of mischief would then break out.

Sadly, Hob and his other goblin friends have gone and we are all poorer by their passing.

The dale is a quiet place and so this walk is one of solitude, but solitude can be pleasant with the right company or state of mind. The walk is peace itself, first through a pastoral valley with an old mill and then high up on to a lovely old coach road across a windswept heather moor, with only the curlews and skylarks for company.

A Bransdale Mill. Coming on this substantial group of industrial buildings in a remote corner of Upper Bransdale is something of a surprise, especially when one takes in their carefully restored state. The mill, owned since 1968 by the National Trust and renovated mainly by the efforts of the Acorn Volunteers, has been here since before the 13th century. Originally it was a soke mill, an unpopular system which gave the miller a lucrative monopoly to mill corn grown locally or brought into the area. The present buildings are mainly 19th-century and date from when it was owned by William Strickland. He changed a simple mill into a complex industrial development. His son Emmanuel Strickland was a man with talents admired in his time; it was Emmanuel who embellished the buildings with classical inscriptions, the most prominent being those on the large plaque above the porch on the east wall. Translated they read as follows:-

In Hebrew : Proverbs Ch.1, v. 7 'The fear of the Lord is the beginning of wisdom'
In Greek : Thessalonians Ch.5, vv 16 and 17 'Always rejoice, pray without ceasing, In everything give thanks.'
In Latin :
'This plaque was set up by me Emmanuel Strickland, B.A. King's College, Cambridge and vicar of Ingleby Greenhow, Cleveland 1837.'

B Viewpoint. The ancient Bransdale church of St Nicholas fits snugly into the dale head setting, sheltered by the forest from the cold winds which blow down from Bransdale Moor.

C Here is the old coach road from Kirkbymoorside to Stokesley and Guisborough. Climbing Rudland Rigg to the south it followed a straight course high above the 1000 feet (305 m) contour for over eight miles. Humps on the near skyline to the west are the tumuli of Three Howes.

D Viewpoint south along the lower valley of Hodge Beck. Known as Bransdale in its upper reaches, it has three identities before linking with the River Dove and then joining the River Rye, flowing south into the Vale of Pickering.

Over

0 _____ 1 mile
0 _____ 1 km

6 Follow the road into a depression and turn right through a field gate on to a grassy track. Climb towards the edge of the pine forest.

7 Leave the forest edge to follow a rough track across the moor.

8 Turn right on to the sandy moorland road.

9 Turn right on a modern track, used as an access road to the moorland shooting butts.

5 Go through the farmyard and then left along the road.

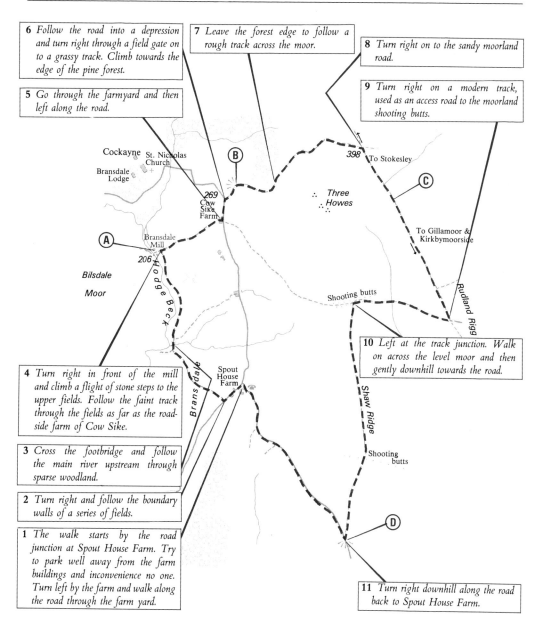

Cockayne   St. Nicholas Church

Bransdale Lodge

Ⓑ

398   To Stokesley

Ⓒ

269 Cow Sike Farm

∴ Three Howes ∴∴

Bransdale Mill

Ⓐ

206

To Gillamoor & Kirkbymoorside

Bilsdale

Moor

Rudland Rigg

Shooting butts

Hodge Beck

10 Left at the track junction. Walk on across the level moor and then gently downhill towards the road.

4 Turn right in front of the mill and climb a flight of stone steps to the upper fields. Follow the faint track through the fields as far as the roadside farm of Cow Sike.

Spout House Farm

Bransdale

Shaw Ridge

3 Cross the footbridge and follow the main river upstream through sparse woodland.

Shooting butts

2 Turn right and follow the boundary walls of a series of fields.

1 The walk starts by the road junction at Spout House Farm. Try to park well away from the farm buildings and inconvenience no one. Turn left by the farm and walk along the road through the farm yard.

Ⓓ

11 Turn right downhill along the road back to Spout House Farm.

27

THORGILL AND BLAKEY RIDGE

6¼ miles (10 km) Moderate / strenuous; 656 feet (200m)

There was once a railway which wound its way all round the skyline of Rosedale, collecting dried ore from kilns near the major ironstone mines, to provide raw material for the blast furnaces of Tees-side. The ore was mostly worked out and the uneconomical mines abandoned by the mid 1920's; since then the dale and its surrounding moors have made a miraculous recovery. No longer do we hear the whistle of the trains as they toil around the head of Rosedale, or see and smell the fumes from drying kilns. The population of the dale has dramatically decreased from what it was a hundred years ago, but stories abound of life in those days, such as of beds in cottages shared by different shifts of miners, which never grew cold. There are still men living in the dale who worked in the mines as boys,

or perhaps remember illicitly riding on the trains. Land which was being soured and spoilt by fumes from the kilns has recovered, and the moor has gone back to its natural state.

The railway track is one of the finest legacies remaining from this long dead industry. With it we can explore the moors in safety without the worry of exact navigation. The cinder track runs from Bank Top in the west, all the way round the eastern arm of Rosedale, to the ruined kilns above Hill Cottages on the Daleside road. A junction near the Lion Inn on Blakey Ridge led the track away to Blowarth Crossing and the Ingleby Incline. This walk only uses about 2½ miles (4 km) of the railway, but an energetic walker could easily follow the complete circuit of track around the 7½

miles (12 km) of skyline from Bank Top to Hill Cottages.

Like many of the walks in this guide, this is one of contrasts. Thorgill, where it starts and finishes, was built on Viking foundations; the sturdy cottages lining its stream - 'gill' is the local term -housed miners who worked beneath the nearby moors in Sheriff's Pit, one of the most important Rosedale ironstone mines. A short but steep climb from Thorgill joins the railway, where the wide level track leads off across the heather moors of Blakey Ridge, passing Sheriff's Pit along the way. A downhill path, away from the railway line, aims for the sheltered lands of the valley bottom where an easy lane runs between ancient field boundaries back to Thorgill.

A Viewpoint across Rosedale, looking over to the eastern arm of the railway. Kilns for drying the ironstone can still be made out above Hill Cottages. Rosedale Moor stretches into the hazy distance.

B Sheriff's Pit, one of the major ironstone mines, is to the left of the track. The ruins are of the pit-head winding gear and also the fenced-off, deeply-flooded mine shaft. Take care around the edge of the shaft and also near any others found on the moors; the sides are crumbling and a slip would mean disaster.

C Viewpoint for upper Rosedale and the moors. The Lion Inn is about three quarters of a mile (1 km) further along the Blakey Ridge road.

Over

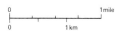

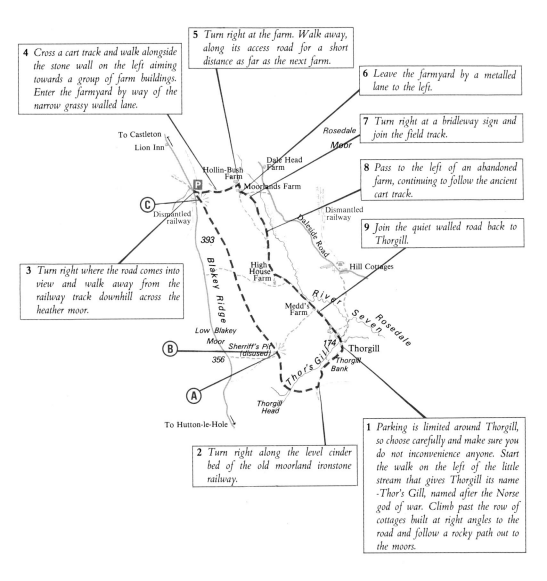

5 *Turn right at the farm. Walk away, along its access road for a short distance as far as the next farm.*

4 *Cross a cart track and walk alongside the stone wall on the left aiming towards a group of farm buildings. Enter the farmyard by way of the narrow grassy walled lane.*

6 *Leave the farmyard by a metalled lane to the left.*

7 *Turn right at a bridleway sign and join the field track.*

8 *Pass to the left of an abandoned farm, continuing to follow the ancient cart track.*

9 *Join the quiet walled road back to Thorgill.*

3 *Turn right where the road comes into view and walk away from the railway track downhill across the heather moor.*

2 *Turn right along the level cinder bed of the old moorland ironstone railway.*

1 *Parking is limited around Thorgill, so choose carefully and make sure you do not inconvenience anyone. Start the walk on the left of the little stream that gives Thorgill its name -Thor's Gill, named after the Norse god of war. Climb past the row of cottages built at right angles to the road and follow a rocky path out to the moors.*

To Castleton
Lion Inn
Hollin-Bush Farm
Dale Head Farm
Moorlands Farm
Rosedale Moor
Dismantled railway
Dismantled railway
Daleside Road
393
Blakey Ridge
High House Farm
Hill Cottages
River Seven
Rosedale
Medd's Farm
Low Blakey Moor
Sherriff's Pit (disused)
356
174
Thorgill
Thorgill Bank
Thor's Gill
To Hutton-le-Hole
Thorgill Head

ROSEDALE ABBEY
4¼ miles (7 km) Moderate

Here we have an all seasons walk. In spring the daffodils rival those of Farndale, but are not so well known and therefore not visited by the same number of people. Autumn sees the moors change to a rich purple when the scent of heather can be almost overpowering. Summer though, cannot be discounted for this is when the high meadows are ready for haymaking and it is then that the field flowers are at their best. Winter, in its turn, brings frost and snow and a grand silence between the storms, when nature tempts the unwary out on to the moors.

Apart from a wall or two and the remains of a tower, all that is left of the abbey, or strictly speaking priory, has been incorporated into Rosedale parish church. Built for Cistercian nuns in 1158 by William of Rosedale, it lasted until 1536 when the edict of Henry VIII spelt its end. The abbey had its own sacred well which can be found inside a low stone shelter standing at the entrance to the nearby campsite.

The valley prospered when ironstone was mined, but with the decline of the industry it has moved back to being a sleepy backwater. Once-polluted streams now sparkle again and forest plantations cloak the hillside, replacing trees cut down to fuel medieval iron furnaces.

When William the Conqueror came north to view his kingdom after the Battle of Hastings, he and his retinue were trapped for several days by a violent storm on the nearby moors. An account of this epic journey describes the moors as though they were alpine peaks; no wonder they were called Blackamore until a century or so ago.

The Rosedale Circuit, a tough 37 mile (59.5 km) walk which crosses nine dales and involves about 5000 feet (1524 m) of climbing, starts and finishes at Rosedale Abbey. Normally the walk takes two days to complete, but it has been done in less.

A Rosedale Abbey. What little remains of this once-proud building has been incorporated into the parish church.

B Viewpoint. Rosedale is in front, with Blakey Ridge filling the skyline.

Over

0   1 mile

0   1 km

4 Turn right at the end of the barn on the right of the road. Follow the signposted bridleway uphill to the open moor.

5 Walk ahead to join a moorland track coming from the left. Keep right at the next fork and aim for the road which will be indicated by passing cars.

6 Cross the road and follow the direction of a signpost pointing the way through the heather. The path is narrow and not well-defined at this point and if you are in any doubt, keep slightly to the left towards the upper road as shown on the map. Turn right on the road and follow it as far as a cattle grid by the forest edge.

3 Join the farm road, turn right and walk as far as a roadside group of farm buildings.

2 Aim uphill towards the ruined barn. Approach it through the gate and turn left to pass the front of the building. Walk away on the right of a field boundary wall.

7 Turn right away from the road at the cattle grid. Go downhill across the rough moor away from the pine forest. Walk towards the near corner of the small plantation lower down the hillside, the plantation will not be immediately apparent.

1 The walk starts in the centre of Rosedale Abbey village. Turn right between the Milburn Arms car park and a converted chapel, then left over a footbridge to walk upstream through a series of meadows, crossing field boundaries by stiles or gates.

Brown Hill

12 Turn right and follow the road back to Rosedale Abbey.

Hartoft Moor

11 Turn right away from the farm and follow a diagonal route over two fields keeping to the right of the modern building close to the road. Go to the right of the house then walk down the drive to the road.

10 Keep left through the farmyard.

9 Turn right across two adjoining stiles and follow yellow waymark arrows towards The Grange Farm. After rain there may be mud in the immediate vicinity of the farmyard.

8 Cross the stile and continue down hill through the lower field alongside a boundary wall.

North Dale

Northdale Rigg

North Dale Beck

Rosedale

Milburn Arms Inn
Rosedale
133 Abbey

The Grange Farm

River Seven

Cattle grid

301

208

A

B

DELVES AND THE
BUTTER BECK VALLEY 2¾ miles (4½ km) Easy / moderate

0   1 mile

0   1 km

Quite often a walk seems to be hiding itself, just waiting to be discovered. This is such a walk: it wanders around the wooded lower reaches of Butter Beck and passes interesting farm buildings. The views are wide, of moor and dale, all helping to make this a most enjoyable and gentle of walks.

The steep road out of Egton Bridge towards Delves, and the start of the walk, is narrow and parking could be a problem. However, there is room for at least three or four cars on the grass verges below the hairpin bends near The Delves, which should be suitable without restricting access.

1 *From the top of the hill, follow the lane opposite Delves Farm to Butter Park and Lodge Hill farms.*

7 *Turn left at the road to climb uphill by the steep hairpin bends to Delves.*

6 *The Delves Farm has considerable architectural merit. built from the warm-hued local stone it makes a pleasing scene as the walker approaches along the nearby field tracks. Turn right here, pass the farm and go out along its access road.*

5 *Cross the footbridge and keep to the left of a small tree-edged stream flowing from The Delves at the top of the field. The banks of the stream are lined with snowdrops in spring.*

2 *Go through Lodge Hill farmyard then left immediately beyond the far gate. Walk steeply downhill, slanting right and between clumps of furze.*

4 *About 150 yards (137 m) beyond Grange Head Farm cross the stile in the wire fence on the left. Keeping the field boundary on the right, walk downhill through sparse scrub to the point where the boundary hedge turns sharply left. There is a gap in the hedge at this point which may be wired off to stop animals from straying. If this is so, climb over or duck under the wire, or otherwise cross the gap. Walk downhill across the open field to the stream in valley bottom.*

3 *Cross the narrow footbridge at the bottom of the slope and walk through sparse woodland with mature plantations on either side. Climb slightly uphill across a series of fields, entering and leaving them by barred gates. At Grange Head Farm follow the farm lane to the left around the side of rough pasture. Continue along the lane following the edge of natural woodland. Pass Hall Grange Farm; downhill to an area of woodland surrounding a narrow valley on the left.*

A *Viewpoint, looking downhill through wooded Butter Beck Valley towards Esk Dale. Egton High Moor rises to your left.*

River Esk

East Arncliff Wood

To Egton Bridge

Delves

71

Delves Farm

The Delves Farm

Hall Grange Farm

Butter Park Farm

Butter Beck

Lodge Hill Farm

Butter Beck

Grange Head Farm

(A)

Egton High Moor

32

ROBIN HOOD'S BAY

2½ miles (4 km) Moderate

0   1 mile

0   1 km

Ever since people have lived in Robin Hood's Bay, they have had the sea as both friend and enemy. Fishing as a full-time occupation is a shadow of its former self, when every able-bodied man in this village earned his living from the sea.

Open to the ravages of storm-pressed seas, the coast has seen many tragedies, but none more horrific than the wrecking of the hospital ship *Rohilla* in 1914, which ran aground between Whitby and Robin Hood's Bay. As well as ship-wreck, houses have been known to disappear during storms when the soft boulder clay of the cliffs is undermined by wave action. Expensive sea defence schemes can only hope to hold back the remorseless attack of the waves for a comparitively short time. The latest scheme, which created an attractive little promenade, was finished in 1975, but is already showing signs of erosion.

Known as the Clovelly of the North, the old part of the village can only be approached on foot. Red-roofed houses crowd each other in a picturesque jumble; a jumble, so local legend has it, caused by newly wed couples never wanting to live far from their parents! All the houses have steep staircases and many have a tiny landing window, said to be designed to allow coffins to be lowered into the street!

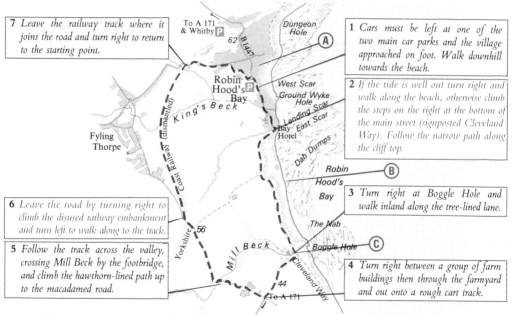

7 *Leave the railway track where it joins the road and turn right to return to the starting point.*

1 *Cars must be left at one of the two main car parks and the village approached on foot. Walk downhill towards the beach.*

2 *If the tide is well out turn right and walk along the beach, otherwise climb the steps on the right at the bottom of the main street (signposted Cleveland Way). Follow the narrow path along the cliff top.*

3 *Turn right at Boggle Hole and walk inland along the tree-lined lane.*

6 *Leave the road by turning right to climb the disused railway embankment and turn left to walk along to the track.*

5 *Follow the track across the valley, crossing Mill Beck by the footbridge, and climb the hawthorn-lined path up to the macadamed road.*

4 *Turn right between a group of farm buildings then through the farmyard and out onto a rough cart track.*

A Spend time exploring the quaint narrow alleys lined with fishermen's cottages. There is no harbour here and boats are launched from the beach or from the main street at high tide. At other stages of the tide fishermen use the shelter of the exposed seaward-curving arms of rock known locally as scars.

B If the tide is out, an alternative will be to walk along the beach parallel to the cliff as far as Boggle Hole. Then time can be spent looking in pools left by the outgoing tide, or searching for the now-rare jet, a form of fossilised wood.

C The mill at Boggle Hole, now a youth hostel, was powered by Mill Beck. A 'boggle' is a Yorkshire name for a sprite or hobgoblin who would help people when treated kindly enough.

RAVENSCAR
5 miles (8 km) Moderate; muddy and slippery sections

During the time of the Roman occupation of Britain there was a lookout and signalling station on the cliff top at Ravenscar. Part of a chain of signal stations linking the north-east coast, it served as the ancient equivalent of the Ballistic Missile Early Warning Station on Fylingdales Moor. Then, as now, there was danger of attack from the north and east; only the technology has changed.

Visitors to Ravenscar, known locally as 'Bay Town', can be forgiven if they note a certain unfinished atmosphere about the place. This is because Ravenscar is a holiday resort which began as a speculative venture and was never quite finished. Once there were grandiose ideas of building another Scarborough here, but the unstable geology of the area and the resulting undermining of the sea cliffs made large-scale building a hazardous proposition. The only building of merit is the Raven Hall Hotel which is built on the site of the Roman signal station. From 1774 it was a private residence and George III was often sent here for treatment during his bouts of madness. In the early 1800s large sums were spent on extending the hall, and the terraced gardens were extended to their present proportions.

Inland and to the west of Ravenscar village there is an extensive area of overgrown quarries. Starting in the early part of the 17th century, vast quantities of alum were quarried and processed by a rather unsavoury alchemy requiring the import of urine collected from the inns and public houses of London. Boats carrying the barrelled urine would beach themselves in partially-made havens below the cliffs and load up with finished alum to sail away on the next high tide. Alum was used as a mordant to 'fix' dyes in woollen cloth. The industry, which ran until about 1871, was started on the instructions of Henry VIII, who wished to break the then papal monopoly of its use in fixing fashionable 'turkey red' dyes. In the early years of this century shale which covered the alum layers, was used for brick-making. Traces of the brick kilns are the only tangible remains of what were once intensively worked quarries.

This is an area of complex geology, mostly from the Jurassic Period of about 160 million years ago. Numerous fault lines and weak strata have left the surrounding land and coast in a state of constant flux. As you walk along the bed of the abandoned Yorkshire Coast Railway you will be conscious of this movement, which shows itself prominently in sudden slopes, far steeper than any track gradient.

There is a Geological Trail through the quarry, covered by an easily understood booklet, which is available from the Ravenscar National Trust Information Centre, or from the North York Moors National Park Office.

A Ravenscar has a number of cafes and restaurants as well as the Raven Hall Hotel, a building of some architectural merit.

B The Geological Trail runs through the quarries, then across the fields below the railway track, as far as the promontory to the seaward side of the Raven Hall Hotel. Fancifully worn rocks and jagged scars reaching out to sea are the uncovered layers of harder strata. The quarry section of the trail can easily be added to this walk and the seaward end followed later.

C Earth movement is noted from the unnatural steepening of the track bed or slumping of land in the fields below and to the right of the railway. When in operation the Yorkshire Coast Railway, which ran from Scarborough to Whitby and Saltburn by the Sea, could boast of being one of the most attractive lines in the North of England.

D Stoupe Beck Sands is an ideal place for a picnic, either on the beach at low tide or on the grassy foreshore above. Difficult road access makes this an almost unknown beach and as a result it is never overcrowded.

Over

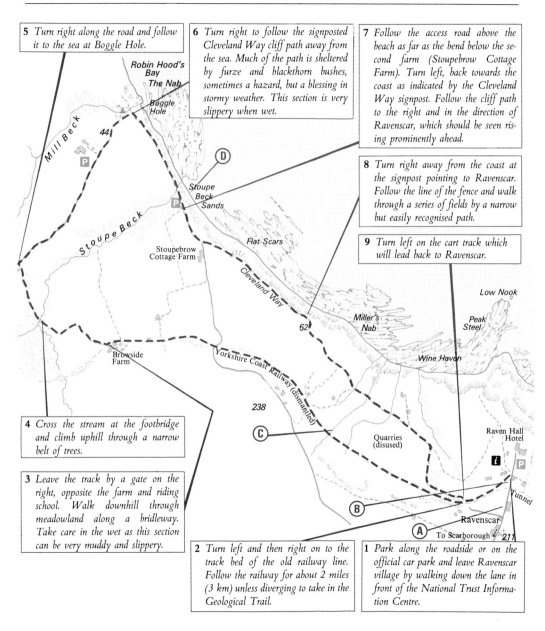

5 Turn right along the road and follow it to the sea at Boggle Hole.

6 Turn right to follow the signposted Cleveland Way cliff path away from the sea. Much of the path is sheltered by furze and blackthorn bushes, sometimes a hazard, but a blessing in stormy weather. This section is very slippery when wet.

7 Follow the access road above the beach as far as the bend below the second farm (Stoupebrow Cottage Farm). Turn left, back towards the coast as indicated by the Cleveland Way signpost. Follow the cliff path to the right and in the direction of Ravenscar, which should be seen rising prominently ahead.

8 Turn right away from the coast at the signpost pointing to Ravenscar. Follow the line of the fence and walk through a series of fields by a narrow but easily recognised path.

9 Turn left on the cart track which will lead back to Ravenscar.

4 Cross the stream at the footbridge and climb uphill through a narrow belt of trees.

3 Leave the track by a gate on the right, opposite the farm and riding school. Walk downhill through meadowland along a bridleway. Take care in the wet as this section can be very muddy and slippery.

2 Turn left and then right on to the track bed of the old railway line. Follow the railway for about 2 miles (3 km) unless diverging to take in the Geological Trail.

1 Park along the roadside or on the official car park and leave Ravenscar village by walking down the lane in front of the National Trust Information Centre.

MAY BECK AND SNEATON HIGH MOOR

9½ miles (15 km) Strenuous with boggy sections. Do not attempt in mist or bad weather

This is a long and tough walk, but one which if undertaken with care and sufficient time, and in good weather, will lead to a true understanding of the moors. The walk is a circuit of the forest which now covers Sneaton High Moor. North of the forest it crosses land belonging to two different types of farm. Both are worth a passing glance. May Beck Farm is a development of the traditional 'long house', a link which goes back to the Viking times. Leas Head Farm is more prosperous and the farmer, a supporter of the local hunt, kennels some of the hounds.

Fylingdales and Sneaton Moors are dotted with tumuli, crosses, standing stones and enigmatic earthworks; many are waymarks on old roads.

A Only the stone base remains of John Cross, a wayside cross of early Christian origins, probably destroyed by puritans in the 17th century. The stone which now fits in the base is of a later date and is the boundary marker between the parishes of Sneaton and Fylingdales.

B The path cuts through four linear mounds of Bronze Age origin; these are thought either to have had religious significance or simply to have been a tribal boundary. On the right are two standing stones, one of which, from one angle, looks like the scrawny neck and face of an old crone, earning it the title 'Old Wife's Neck'.

C The prominent cross and cairn about 44 yards (40 m) south of the guide post mark the tumulus of Lilla Howe, and the grave of Lilla, a servant who gave his life in AD626 to save the King of Northumberland. The cross is thought to be the oldest local Christian symbol.

D Ann's Cross is one of the countless standing stones and crosses marking the moorland heights.

E Whinstone Ridge, an arrow-straight intrusion of basalt occurring between Esk Dale and Fylingdales Moor.

F Falling Foss, an attractive waterfall in a woodland setting, is slightly off the route of this walk.

Over

36

0 ┣━━━━━━━━━━┫ 1 mile
0 ┣━━━━━━━━━━┫ 1 km

14 *Go to the right of the farm buildings along a cart track. Cross a small tree-lined stream and climb by the side of the next field, gradually swinging left to join another track.*

13 *Join the bridleway bearing right for Leas Head Farm.*

12 *Go through the gate away from the moor and cross a series of fields. Take care to close all gates to prevent stock from straying.*

11 *Cross the rocky stream bed and climb, to the right, through heather, as far as a footpath junction. Turn right and walk downstream, keeping a level course above the steepest part of the valley.*

15 *Aim for the group of barns shown on the map as Foss Farm. Go downhill along the farm lane by the side of a holly hedge on the right, marking the forest boundary.*

16 *Turn right along the waymarked forest trail and follow its signs through a mixture of natural and planted woodlands.*

17 *Keep left at the junction of paths to follow the Forest Walk back to May Beck car park.*

1 *From May Beck car park walk back along the access road for about 100 yards (91 m).*

2 *Turn right by May Beck Trail waymark number 1 and climb through bracken and rough pasture to the field fence. Turn left along this fence as far as a stile. N.B. Do not worry if you cannot find the path in its early stages: it is probably lost under the quickly growing bracken.*

3 *Cross the stile and turn right along a moorland track.*

4 *Go through the gate in the boundary fence near John Cross (N.B. ignore the path following the forest boundary) and walk for about 60 yards (55 m) along the track. Turn right on to a narrow path through the heather. Look for waymarks numbered 6 to 9 as a guide for this part of the walk.*

5 *Walk ahead on the central of three tracks away from marker number 9. Climb gently uphill through the heather, occasionally walking round or even wading through short stretches of peat bog. As the path is indistinct in places, try to keep about 200 yards (183 m) from the edge of the forest, which should always be to your right.*

10 *Right at a boundary stone and away from the forestry road, by path across a stretch of boggy moorland.*

9 *Turn left at the junction with the forestry road.*

8 *Do not go through the gate, but keep left on the moorland track.*

7 *Turn right at the guide post and stone cairn on to a gravel track; head north west across the highest and most open section of the moor.*

6 *Ignore a path on your left, continue to walk ahead along a gentle rise.*

Walk 18

MALLYAN SPOUT AND THE GOATHLAND HISTORIC RAILWAY 3½ miles (5½ km) Easy

Goathland is a place where the breezes always seem to blow; the main village straggles along the road above Eller Beck, but the upper village is clustered around its open common, where grazing sheep come right up to cottage doors.

The railway was first opened to horse-drawn trains in 1836, when George Stephenson laid a track from Whitby to Pickering. South of Grosmont, technical problems meant that the line had to climb high above the river in the space of three miles. The only way to climb the 197 feet (60 m) to Goathland was to haul rolling stock by wire rope, up the 1 in 15 incline from Beck Hole. Despite many modifications, the line was unsatisfactory and in 1865 a 'Deviation Line', was blasted through solid rock along the present route now used by the North York Moors Railway.

7 *Turn right at the top of the incline on the road back to the car park. Travellers on the North York Moors Railway will have to turn left beyond the car park for the road back to Goathland Station.*

1 *Park on the upper car park, or walk up the road from Goathland Station if travelling by train.*

6 *Turn right at Beck Hole cottages and climb the tree-lined cinder bed of the incline and walk along the route of the dismantled railway.*

5 *Turn left at the river to reach Mallyan Spout. Return to this point afterwards; the walk continues downstream on a clearly defined footpath, crossing field boundaries by stiles and following the edge of the wooded ravine of West Beck.*

4 *Cross the common to the Mallyan Hotel. Take the signposted path downhill to the right of the hotel. Follow it through a narrow belt of trees into the wooded valley. N.B. This is a popular footpath which can be very muddy and slippery after rain.*

3 *Turn right at Abbot's House Camp Site and follow the signposted path through the field. Cross a small stream by the footbridge and walk through a series of fields alongside a plantation of mature pines.*

2 *Turn right at the Goathland Hotel (left if coming from the station) and walk along the cinder track of the old railway.*

A Mallyan Spout. The path to the 70 ft (21 m) high waterfall is over smooth boulders, often slippery.

B The Incline. Coaches and wagons were hauled up by a wire rope. Notice the attractive architecture of the track-side cottages at Beck Hole and also at the top of the incline. There is a short piece of the original iron rail on its stone block sleepers, outside Incline Cottages at Beck Hole.

CLOUGHTON AND
HAYBURN WYKES   4½ miles (7 km) Moderate

0 _____ 1 mile
0 _____ 1 km

'Wyke' is the Yorkshire dialect word for a small sheltered bay. Both wykes visited on this walk make ideal picnic spots. Cloughton Wyke is popular with sea anglers who can cast their lines from the rocks into the deep inshore waters. Close by, the name 'Salt Pans' is probably a relic of the process of evaporating sea water to make salt. Although nothing can now be seen to verify this theory, salt was a valuable commodity in fishing communities as a

means of preserving the catch.

The approach to Hayburn Wyke is through a fairy-like dell and on to a rocky beach, where the stones offer up fossils of long dead plants and sea creatures. A stream flowing through the woods cascades to the beach in a tiny waterfall, completing the scene. The woodlands and cove of Hayburn Wyke are owned by the Yorkshire Naturalists' Trust, but public access is free on the understanding that

respect is paid to plant life and no damage is done to the rocks.

This walk is in two distinct sections: the first is along the coast with tantalising views of inaccessible rocky beaches below a sometimes dangerously crumbling cliff. From Hayburn Wyke, the return climbs gently through woodland to reach the railway track where nature has converted a man-made route into a pleasantly wooded path.

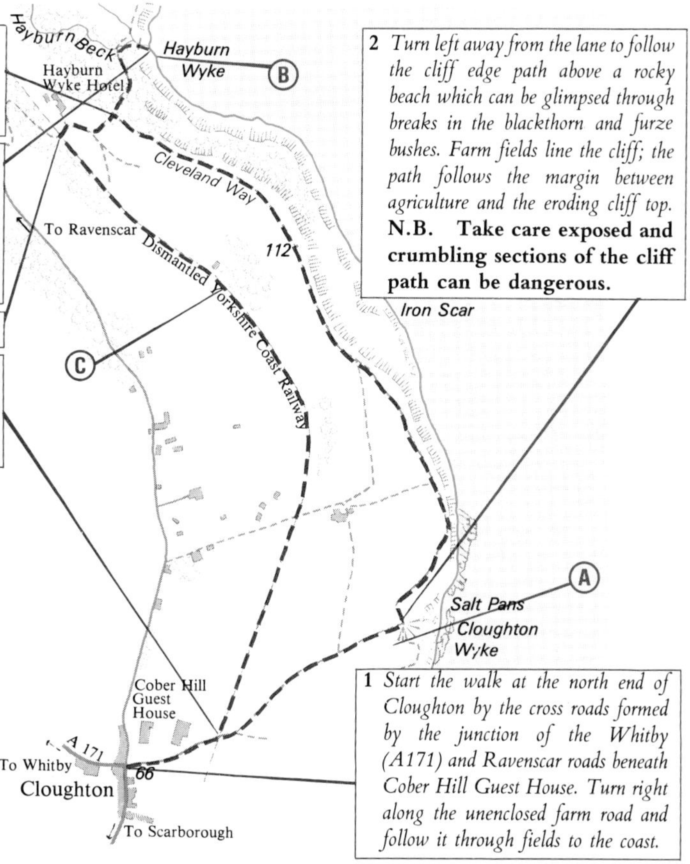

3 *Turn right at the footpath junction and walk down through the woods to Hayburn Wyke. Climb down to the beach by the side of the waterfall.*

4 *Return to the footpath junction, climb through the wood, then across the corner of a small field to the Hayburn Wyke Hotel. Take the hotel access road, to the left, as far as the Yorkshire Coast Railway track.*

5 *Turn left along the railway bed.*

6 *Climb a short flight of steps by the side of the bridge. Turn right along the lane to return to the Cober Hill Guest House and Cloughton village.*

2 *Turn left away from the lane to follow the cliff edge path above a rocky beach which can be glimpsed through breaks in the blackthorn and furze bushes. Farm fields line the cliff; the path follows the margin between agriculture and the eroding cliff top.* **N.B. Take care exposed and crumbling sections of the cliff path can be dangerous.**

A A small car park gives sea anglers easy access to Cloughton Wyke.

B A perfect spot for a picnic on a warm sunny day. Fossils can be found among the pebbles on the beach. The wooded dell above is a riot of bluebells, anemones and celandines, and other woodland flowers, in late spring.

C Notice how scrub willow and birch colonise the track sides.

1 *Start the walk at the north end of Cloughton by the cross roads formed by the junction of the Whitby (A171) and Ravenscar roads beneath Cober Hill Guest House. Turn right along the unenclosed farm road and follow it through fields to the coast.*

Map labels: Hayburn Beck · Hayburn Wyke · Hayburn Wyke Hotel · Cleveland Way · To Ravenscar · Dismantled Yorkshire Coast Railway · 112 · Iron Scar · Salt Pans · Cloughton Wyke · Cober Hill Guest House · To Whitby · A171 · 66 · Cloughton · To Scarborough

Walk 20
REASTY BANK AND
WHISPER DALES   4 miles (6 km) Easy; one short uphill section

0   1 mile
0   1 km

Quite often a romantically sounding place name can prove to be a disappointment and anyone visiting this area for the first time can be excused a passing cynicism at the name Whisper Dales. However, here the name fits the situation and Whisper Dales once discovered remains as a pleasurable memory for a long time. The road from Scarborough follows the edge of a north-east-facing escarpment where the gentle south-west slopes are clothed in planta- tions of mixed conifers. Deep valleys bite into the escarpment, and prosperous farms make the most of the shelter offered by forest and a sunny aspect. The ambience of silent forest and farmland is, with the exception of the architecture, reminiscent of the Black Forest in Germany. From the car park on Reasty Bank the view northwards is of the upper reaches of the Derwent, with tantalising glimpses of the vast expanse of Fylingdales Moor, appear- ing between the arms of Harwood Dale and Langdale Forests. Waymarked Forest Trails start from Reasty Bank, and also a complex network of forest roads and firebreaks making it possible to wander for hours on end with only birdsong and the scent of pines for company. This walk follows a series of forest tracks and visits two of the most attractive side valleys in the upper Derwent; it is a walk of contrasts and ever-changing views.

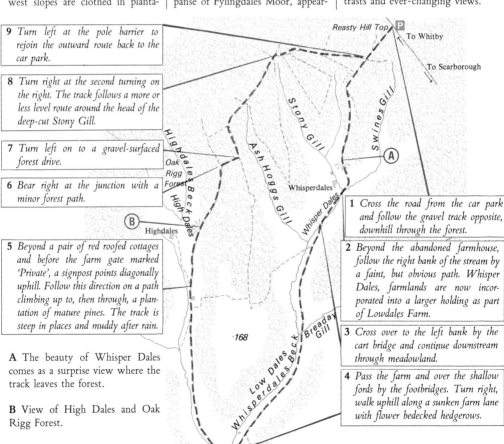

9 Turn left at the pole barrier to rejoin the outward route back to the car park.

8 Turn right at the second turning on the right. The track follows a more or less level route around the head of the deep-cut Stony Gill.

7 Turn left on to a gravel-surfaced forest drive.

6 Bear right at the junction with a minor forest path.

5 Beyond a pair of red roofed cottages and before the farm gate marked 'Private', a signpost points diagonally uphill. Follow this direction on a path climbing up to, then through, a plantation of mature pines. The track is steep in places and muddy after rain.

A The beauty of Whisper Dales comes as a surprise view where the track leaves the forest.

B View of High Dales and Oak Rigg Forest.

1 Cross the road from the car park and follow the gravel track opposite, downhill through the forest.

2 Beyond the abandoned farmhouse, follow the right bank of the stream by a faint, but obvious path. Whisper Dales, farmlands are now incorporated into a larger holding as part of Lowdales Farm.

3 Cross over to the left bank by the cart bridge and continue downstream through meadowland.

4 Pass the farm and over the shallow fords by the footbridges. Turn right, walk uphill along a sunken farm lane with flower bedecked hedgerows.

40

Walk 21
FORGE VALLEY
3½ miles (5½ km) Moderate

Here is nature's engineering on the grand scale. The deeply wooded gorge of Forge Valley is the 'unnatural' route of the Derwent, its real course being that now used by the flood prevention scheme known as the Sea Cut, which follows a wide valley bottom in a direct line to the sea. Towards the end of the last Ice Age, when the still frozen North Sea held back melt waters from the land, the Derwent had nowhere to go other than through a narrow side valley to the south.

Such was the volume of water flowing through this minor valley that it deepened and when the sea eventually thawed, the river continued on its new course, flooding what is now the Vale of Pickering. The Sea Cut, dug in the mid 19th century, reduced the danger of flooding and greatly improved land in the vale.

Forge Valley has been designated a National Nature Reserve to conserve its natural beauty. Its trees are mostly deciduous, growing on an alkaline soil based on the underlying oolitic limestone. Woodland flowers, such as anemones, bluebells and primroses, flourish in their season, and on the riverbanks the bright golden yellow of marsh marigolds makes a brave show in late spring.

Farmland fills the woldlike plateaux above the valley sides where rolling acres of cereal crops make a sharp contrast to the damp and shady environment of the valley bottom.

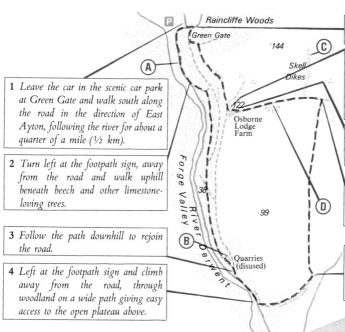

1 Leave the car in the scenic car park at Green Gate and walk south along the road in the direction of East Ayton, following the river for about a quarter of a mile (½ km).

2 Turn left at the footpath sign, away from the road and walk uphill beneath beech and other limestone-loving trees.

3 Follow the path downhill to rejoin the road.

4 Left at the footpath sign and climb away from the road, through woodland on a wide path giving easy access to the open plateau above.

5 At the junction of field tracks, turn sharp left on to a sunken track, following it as far as the belt of trees seen ahead on the near skyline.

6 Turn left on an unmetalled farm lane and walk towards a group of farm buildings.

7 At the farmyard take the first gate on the right and make your way to the left, round the back of the farm.

8 Go through a gate in the boundary wall between farm and woodland. Turn right and follow the footpath, descending through woodland as far as the road.

9 Turn left along the road, to reach the car park.

A Behind the roadside well, a small stone hut housed a hydraulic ram, to lift water to farms on the dry plateau to the east.

B Warm hues in the quarry face are of oolite, a fine grained limestone. The name 'oolite' comes from the Greek word for fish roe.

C The tree-covered walls of Skell Dikes are a prehistoric boundary.

D Viewpoint over the Vale of Pickering with the Wolds beyond.

HACKNESS AND THE DERWENT VALLEY
5¾ miles (9¼ km) Moderate; muddy at first along the river bank

This is a walk which should have something to interest everyone. Woodlands lead to a narrow belt of water-meadow where a uniquely dividing river marks the crux of a nineteenth century flood prevention scheme. It led to the improvement and later prosperity of farms on either side of the Derwent in the Vale of Pickering. An unspoilt village supports the Georgian splendour of a stately home. A short climb through secluded woodland leads to easy heights where the wold-like vista of sky, broad farmland and wood-crowned hills make the foreground to distant moors, completing a scene of rural charm.

St Hilda had a monastic cell built here in 680 AD, as a place of relaxation for the nuns and monks from the main abbey at Whitby. No doubt they thought themselves secure at Hackness when Whitby came under seaborne attack, but in 867 it was destroyed by the Danes. Rebuilt in 1095 it lasted until the Dissolution of 1539. Nothing remains of this holy house except its pond and a small piece of Saxon Cross, now in the church. Here was an idyllic and far more sheltered setting than wild Whitby and it seems strange that the site was abandoned.

The first thing to catch the eye when visiting Hackness village is a shallow guttered stream which seems to flow from beneath a bridge support. Before piped water supplies, the stream provided clean drinking water for the locals and was quite a rarity in the days before the problems of waterborne diseases were fully understood.

The sunny aspect of Hackness Hall speaks eloquently of careful planning by its architect, John Carr of York. This fine example of a Georgian manor house is the home of Lord Derwent.

A The weir marks the start of the Sea Cut, taking excess water eastwards along the original, pre-Ice Age, course of the Derwent.

B Hackness village pond marks the site of St Hilda's monastery. Fish would have been bred in it as a source of food for the nuns and monks.

C The view is of Hackness village, beyond which a series of deep-cut little valleys rise to forested Silpho Moor and Reasty Bank.

D The shallow ditch supported on one side by a low wall, is called a 'ha-ha', designed to keep animals away from the vicinity of the manor house, whilst allowing an unrestricted view across the park.

Over

3 *If there is no stile at this point, either climb the fence following the waymark arrows, or go through the field gate about 100 yards (91 m) uphill to the left. Follow the fence back downhill to regain the route.*

4 *Go through the farmyard at Cockrah House and out the macadamed lane.*

5 *Turn right by a group of cottages, walk down the lane and turn left over a stile immediately before the road bridge. Follow river bank upstream.*

6 *Turn right to cross the river at the footbridge and then over the road to a narrow gate by a footpath sign. There is no obvious track in the field beyond the gate, but the route zig-zags, first to the right and then left up to and along the edge of the belt of woodland at the top of slope.*

7 *Turn right along the metalled road for about 100 yards (91 m) and then right again uphill across a small field and into a dry valley surrounded by natural woodland. Go through the gate on to a narrow path which improves as it climbs. The path leaves the confines of the trees beyond an abandoned lime kiln.*

8 *Walk ahead on to farm access road — signposted to Suffield Ings Farm.*

9 *Go to the left of the farm buildings and then follow the right-hand side of the field boundary, heading towards a narrow belt of woodland above the Derwent valley. Turn right and walk downhill through the trees.*

10 *The route opens out on to a field which may be ploughed. If this is so and the path is indistinct, walk ahead and downhill in single file, towards a white-painted metal gate on the far side.*

11 *Follow the right-hand side of an ancient hawthorne hedge, directly towards a group of farm buildings.*

12 *Go through the farmyard and out on to the road. Turn left and follow the road all the way back to the car park in Forge Valley.*

2 *The path crosses water-meadows and is indistinct in places, but the route follows an almost straight line with the river always in sight on the right.*

1 *The walk starts from the riverside car park in Forge Valley. Cross the upper of the two footbridges and turn right along the riverside path. Duckboards avoid most muddy sections; yellow arrows mark the way.*

Hackness
Hackness Hall
58
Wrench Green
Cockrah House
69
Suffield Ings Farm
159
River Derwent
Weir
Sea Cut
41
Mowthorpe Farm
Forge Valley

Walk 23

BRIDESTONES AND
DALBY FOREST 1 mile (1½ km) Easy

There are numerous Bridestones throughout the North York Moors; no one can say for certain where the title comes from, but it is a fair guess to suggest that they have connections with ancient fertility rites.

The Bridestones, the highpoint in more than one sense of this walk, are a curious geological feature. Sandstone, deposited in a river delta millions of years ago, outcrops above Dove Dale and, due to differences in the hardness of various rock layers, weather action has sculptured the rocks into their present shapes. Set high above the dale with acres of heather moor at their back, both Low and High Bridestones make attractive groupings, obvious vantage points which naturally focus attention as one walks towards them.

Woodland below the Bridestones and also lining the west of Dove Dale is entirely natural, composed mostly of birch and native Scots pines. It is practically the only enclave of natural woodland in thousands of acres of foreign pines planted by the Forestry Commission.

Owned by the National Trust and administered jointly with the Yorkshire Naturalists' Trust, Bridestones Moor and Dove Dale Woods are open to public access, on the understanding that we keep to the paths and do not damage any of the growing trees or pick flowers — which includes heather!

The Forestry Commission have established a toll road through Dalby Forest. The narrow, well-maintained road wanders through miles of pine forest as far as Langdale, near Hackness, in the Derwent valley. Scenic car parks, picnic sites, forest walks and an interpretative Forest Visitor Centre at Low Dalby, are among the facilities to be enjoyed.

4 Turn left away from High Bridestones and walk down the steep slope of Needle Point, a heather-covered ridge separating the twin valleys of Dove Dale Griff and Bridestones Griff.

5 Cross the narrow stream and walk along its right hand bank.

6 Turn left to recross the stream by a small footbridge, go through the wooden squeezer stile into the field and follow the lower edge of the natural woodland.

3 On reaching open moorland turn left on a well established path aiming for the outcrop of Low Bridestones. Follow the path around the head of Bridestones Griff to High Bridestones.

2 Turn right and climb uphill, with occasional yellow waymarks on wooden posts to indicate the route.

7 Leave the field through another squeezer stile and turn right on to the outward path to return car park.

1 Park at the Staindale Water picnic area; cross the road and walk towards the pine trees of the nature reserve.

A Low Bridestones. A series of weather-worn outcropping rocks. Good all round views of forest and moor.

B High Bridestones. Views of Dove Dale and Newgate Moor.

C Bridestones Nature Reserve.

WHINNY NAB

3½ miles (5.6 km) Easy

```
0                                          1 mile
|----------|----------|----------|----------|
0                          1 km
```

The pressures of intensive farming and forest planting on the natural moorland are highlighted on this walk. A short and easy walk, but one which is marked by contrasts, be they the view of the deep Hole of Horcum or the sharp edge of mature forest on Blakey Rigg to the north east. The contrasts come suddenly on the senses, some are natural and pleasing, but others like

the Early Warning Station on Fylingdales Moor are not always so pleasant.

Two ancient tracks are used; both keep to the edge of high escarpments and offer vantage points with far-ranging views. The purpose of these old ways was to take salt to the coast and preserved fish back inland. Saltergate Brow, between

Gallows Dike, above the Hole of Horcum, and Whinny Nab, indicates its previous use, but who the old woman was, who is remembered by the Old Wife's Way, has never been recorded. It is possible that she was a tinker woman, who sold her small but essential trinkets and ribbons to farmers' wives across the moor.

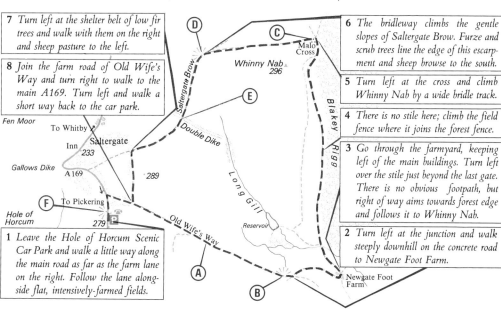

7 *Turn left at the shelter belt of low fir trees and walk with them on the right and sheep pasture to the left.*

8 *Join the farm road of Old Wife's Way and turn right to walk to the main A169. Turn left and walk a short way back to the car park.*

6 *The bridleway climbs the gentle slopes of Saltergate Brow. Furze and scrub trees line the edge of this escarpment and sheep browse to the south.*

5 *Turn left at the cross and climb Whinny Nab by a wide bridle track.*

4 *There is no stile here; climb the field fence where it joins the forest fence.*

3 *Go through the farmyard, keeping left of the main buildings. Turn left over the stile just beyond the last gate. There is no obvious footpath, but right of way aims towards forest edge and follows it to Whinny Nab.*

2 *Turn left at the junction and walk steeply downhill on the concrete road to Newgate Foot Farm.*

1 *Leave the Hole of Horcum Scenic Car Park and walk a little way along the main road as far as the farm lane on the right. Follow the lane alongside flat, intensively-farmed fields.*

Map labels: Fen Moor · To Whitby · Inn · Saltergate 233 · Gallows Dike · A169 · 289 · To Pickering · Hole of Horcum 279 · Saltergate Brow · Whinny Nab 296 · Malo Cross · Double Dike · Blakey Rigg · Long Gill · Reservoir · Old Wife's Way · Newgate Foot Farm · D · C · E · F · A · B

A Old Wife's Way, an ancient pack horse track.

B The land falls steeply into Long Gill, a deep defile scoured by overflowing melt water at the end of the last Ice Age. Beyond, Blakey Topping stands above Allerston and Langdale Forests.

C Malo Cross, an ancient way mark on the salt way to Whitby. The view to the north is of Fylingdales Moor and the complex radar equipment of the Ministry of Defence.

D The view here is across Fen Moor and the deep trough of Newton Dale with Wheeldale

Moor beyond.

E Twin furrows mark the line of Double Dike, a Bronze Age boundary which links Long Gill to the escarpment of Saltergate Brow.

F Viewpoint. The deep gorge of the Hole of Horcum opens up beyond the road.

THE HOLE OF HORCUM

8 miles (13 km) Moderate/strenuous

Escaping torrents from the ice-blocked lake which once filled Esk Dale carved out the deep ravines of the Hole of Horcum and Newton Dale. Both places are seen on this walk; the Hole itself is traversed throughout its length, and Newton Dale can be appreciated from a high vantage point towards the end of the walk.

The Hole of Horcum is a mysterious place and it is easy to imagine that it was once the home of a giant. Folk tales handed down through the centuries speak of the activities of this giant Horcum, who, the ancients believed, had carved his home deep in this moorland cleft. Did these tales begin in the mists of time when the first settlers came to the moors and did they hold strange rites centred around their religious sites perched above the Hole? We cannot say for sure, but it is possible that the myths of today are corruptions of stories handed down by word of mouth since prehistoric times.

This is an exciting walk, starting as it does by descending steeply from the bustle of the Whitby road into the tranquillity of the Hole. A steady climb reaches Levisham, where the road in or out means a climb of 1 in 3. It is a village with proud and hospitable traditions, where they still dance in summer around a maypole in front of the village pub. A long easy track on a springy peat base leads across Levisham Moor where there are dozens of places and objects to tempt walkers away from the main route. One of the diversions follows the line of an earth dyke built for some unknown purpose thousands of years ago. It ends abruptly on top of West Side Brow, high above Newton Dale, where the view is one which should appeal to everyone, old and young. Forest and moor stretch in all directions and the occasional steam train, chugging its way along the dale bottom, comes as a pleasant contrast.

Levisham has its own little halt on the North York Moors Railway, which makes it possible to begin the walk by a train journey. If this alternative is planned it will be necessary to amend the described route by walking from the train to Levisham and then joining and finishing this walk at point number 9 on the map. If you have a train to catch and it means shortening the walk, then a right turn at point number 5 should cut out a couple of miles. This short-cut entails a steep climb up Dundale Griff to Dundale Pond and then over Levisham Moor back to Newton Dale.

A Viewpoint. To the north, the moors are a purple sea of heather in autumn.

B Viewpoint of the Hole of Horcum.

C The local name for a side valley is a 'griff'. The main one is Dundale Griff with its curiously-named tributary, Pigtrough Griff. It is possible to shorten the walk at point 5 by climbing Dundale Griff and rejoining the main route at Dundale Pond (point E), but this would mean missing a possible refreshment stop at Levisham village.

D Levisham village. Trim cottages and farm houses line the wide grassy verges of this isolated village. Good food and refreshments are available at the Horseshoe Inn at the far end of the single village street. There is a small general store and post office.

E Dundale Pond, a comparative rarity on the well-drained moors.

F An ancient boundary dyke leads to a 'Surprise View' on the moor edge high above Newton Dale. Mile upon mile of dense forests stretch away to the west and steam trains may be seen like tiny models way below on the winding track through the narrow dale.

G Oblong patches of heather, known as 'swiddens', have been deliberately burned in rotation to encourage the growth of young heather shoots, to supply food for the grouse kept on this moor for sporting purposes.

Over

0 _____ 1 mile
0 _____ 1 km

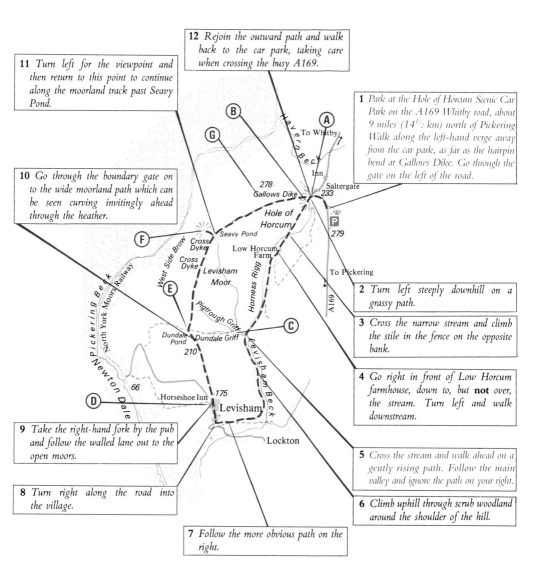

11 Turn left for the viewpoint and then return to this point to continue along the moorland track past Seavy Pond.

12 Rejoin the outward path and walk back to the car park, taking care when crossing the busy A169.

1 Park at the Hole of Horcum Scenic Car Park on the A169 Whitby road, about 9 miles (14½ km) north of Pickering Walk along the left-hand verge away from the car park, as far as the hairpin bend at Gallows Dike. Go through the gate on the left of the road.

10 Go through the boundary gate on to the wide moorland path which can be seen curving invitingly ahead through the heather.

2 Turn left steeply downhill on a grassy path.

3 Cross the narrow stream and climb the stile in the fence on the opposite bank.

4 Go right in front of Low Horcum farmhouse, down to, but **not** over, the stream. Turn left and walk downstream.

9 Take the right-hand fork by the pub and follow the walled lane out to the open moors.

5 Cross the stream and walk ahead on a gently rising path. Follow the main valley and ignore the path on your right.

8 Turn right along the road into the village.

6 Climb uphill through scrub woodland around the shoulder of the hill.

7 Follow the more obvious path on the right.

Map labels: To Whitby, Haven Beck, Inn, Saltergate, 278, Gallows Dike, 233, Hole of Horcum, 279, Seavy Pond, Low Horcum Farm, Cross Dyke, Cross Dyke, Low Horcum, West Side Brow, Levisham Moor, Horness Rigg, To Pickering, A169, Pigtrough Griff, North York Moors Railway, Pickering Beck, Dundale Pond, Dundale Griff, 210, Levisham Beck, Newton Dale, 66, Horseshoe Inn, 175, Levisham, Lockton

Walk 26
LOCKTON-FOUR DALES WALK
5 miles (8 km) Moderate; one steep uphill section 426 feet (130 m)

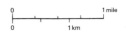

Lockton is a pleasant little village just far enough away from the busy A169 to be unaffected by its traffic. The walk takes us down through Levisham Dale, the first of the four dales, then into Newton Dale where steam trains thread their way from Pickering to Grosmont. A short but steep climb up Cross Dale and a stretch of farmland and forest on either side of the A169 leads to Dalby Dale.

1 *The walk starts by Lockton Church. Walk along the village street ignoring the Levisham turning. Turn right between the last two houses on to a signposted path.*

2 *Go left along Levisham Dale crest.*

3 *Follow the zig-zag path downhill.*

4 *Turn left on a bridle path through woodland.*

5 *Left across the narrow field below the edge of the wood into Newton Dale.*

6 *Climb steeply to the left up the dry valley of Cross Dale.*

7 *Keep to right of farm at valley head aim towards a walled track.*

8 *Join farm lane, walk onto main road.*

9 *Cross the road and follow footpath signs between the Fox Rabbit Farm buildings. Walk away from the farm by the path, as indicated by signs around field boundaries.*

10 *Turn right at bottom corner of last field, cross wall into forest, walk along the fire break into Dalby Dale.*

11 *Go left on to a wide ride, by a green waymarked post.*

12 *Cross over the forestry road and follow the river bank upstream.*

13 *Go left in front of the main building of Staindale Lodge, through a gateway and out on to a woodland path. Follow this uphill to climb beyond the trees, then between a series of fields as far as the main road.*

14 *Cross the road with care and walk down the lane opposite to Lockton.*

To Whitby

Newton-on-Rawcliffe

Levisham

Levisham Mill Farm

Beck

Lockton

B **A**

Staindale Lodge

Low Dalby

C

Farwath

P **Dalby Forest**

Fox & Rabbit Inn & Farm

Pickering Beck

Newton Dale

North Yorkshire Moors Railway

A 169

To Pickering

A A plaque tucked away on the side of a house on the left, below the church, commemorates the building of a well in 1697. The names of eight benefactors were recorded and one has obviously been removed; does this hide a local quarrel, or simply an error? Water is still a valuable commodity on this dry upland plateau and today it has to be pumped to a storage tank.

B Viewpoint. Below is the tiny church which serves Levisham.

There was once a thriving community living around a mill in the valley bottom.

C A good place to watch steam trains below in Newton Dale.

48

PICKERING AND
NEWTON DALE   6¼ miles (10 km) Easy

Pickering, gateway to the moors, is a bustling town where tourism and the day to day business of farming happily coexist.

The old town developed around its castle, standing on the east bank of Pickering Beck, built to control movement between the Vale of Pickering and the moors. There is an even older fortress site on Beacon Hill to the west, but the eastern castle had the better view. There is no history of any conflict over the ownership of Pickering Castle, in fact it seems to have been mostly used as a hunting lodge and somewhere for English kings to rest after their battles with the Scots. Edward II hid here after being trounced at Byland in 1322.

The walk described here is popular locally. It has the advantage of starting from the town centre and quickly reaches out to quiet fields. The deep, wooded valley of Newton Dale leads back to the railway station, with its carefully preserved relics of steam.

8 Go through a gate on to the macadamed farm road and almost immediately turn left through a gate; recross both the railway and river. Aim towards woodland on the far side of the field and turn right along its edge to walk across the meadow.

9 Cross the road, river and railway by the footbridge at the side of a group of cottages.

10 Turn left beyond the last cottage on to a farm lane.

11 Fork left on the field path, down to and then along the river bank. Cross the railway above the station.

7 Turn left, parallel to the railway, along the forest track.

6 Cross Pickering Beck by the footbridge and then over the railway. Take care, listen for approaching trains.

5 Bear left at the junction of footpaths, continuing to walk downhill.

4 Go left through the gate, then downhill on a woodland path confined between an old wall and a wire fence.

3 Climb the stile and cross the field by footpath. Aim towards upper edge of the wood on the opposite side, then turn right following its boundary.

2 Fork left by the old peoples' sheltered accommodation and follow the narrow lane known locally as Love Lane, past the nursery garden towards open fields.

12 Turn right on the road past Pickering Station back to the town centre.

1 Park in one of the central car parks and make your way to the traffic island where the Scarborough (A170) and Whitby (A169) roads cross. Walk up the Whitby road.

A Pickering Station — terminus and headquarters of the North York Moors Railway. Also Information Centre.

B Beck Isle Museum of local history.
C Pickering Castle — 12th century. Access is by way of the narrow lane a few yards below point 12 opposite the station.

D Trout ponds, where for a fee you may catch your own fish.

HUTTON-LE-HOLE

4 miles (6 km) Easy

0   1 mile
0   1 km

The houses of Hutton-le-Hole are scattered at random around its green and Hutton Beck tumbles through their midst in a series of short waterfalls. Sheep graze on either side of the unfenced road and complete a scene which has been featured on many calendars and in countless photographs. The imaginative open-air Ryedale Folk Museum has been developed to one side of the main street. Covering two and a half acres, local antiques and crafts are on display in the open air or in restored farm buildings, some of which have been moved here from places throughout the moors.

3 *Where road bends sharply right, turn left away from it on to a rough track at the side of a swampy field.*

2 *Turn right on the road and walk along its wide grassy verge.*

1 *From the car park, walk to the Information Centre and then go past the chapel. Turn left at a footpath sign and keep to the left of the bowling green. Cross a series of fields and Fairy Call Beck.*

5 *Turn right at a footpath junction to join the lane into Lastingham village.*

4 *Fork right following a well-defined path out on to the open moor. Keep the boundary wall in sight a few yards to your right and walk as far as the group of buildings of Camomile Farm. Turn left away from the farm, still following the wall, to cross a small but steep-sided valley.*

6 *Pass a row of riverside cottages, fork right beyond the last one and walk up the steep grassy track. The track can be muddy after rain, but with a little care the worst parts can be avoided.*

11 *Go downhill through sparse woodland to the roadside. Hutton village is on the right.*

9 *Follow direction signs through the farmyard.*

10 *Follow a waymarked path around the edge of a series of fields.*

7 *Climb through a belt of mature beech trees as far as the road. Turn half right, and walk through Spaunton.*

8 *Turn right at the 'T' junction and then left to Grange Farm.*

A Ryedale Folk Museum.

B Lastingham. Not so well known as Hutton-le-Hole, but arguably more attractive with old houses grouped together along two streets. There was a Benedictine Abbey here, built on Celtic foundations, but it was destroyed by the Danes in 862. It lay in ruins until monks from Whitby temporarily re-established it in 1078, before moving to York in 1086. They left a fine Norman crypt, which is under the present church. There are two irreverent local stories connected with this church. One is that a vicar once used a carved oak server as firewood to melt lead from the church roof. The other concerns the crypt, which was used for cockfighting in the 18th century.

C Viewpoint. Spaunton Moor and Blakey Ridge to the left, a blaze of colour in the autumn, climb in rolling waves beyond the intervening valley.

D Good view of Hutton-le-Hole.

Walk 29
FARNDALE

0 _____ 1 mile
0 _____ 1 km

3¾ miles(6 km) Easy; muddy after heavy rain

The twists and turns of the River Dove have created numerous little wooded dells and above it are glimpses of the high moors. This walk is simple to follow; on the outward leg to Church Houses the river bank keeps the walker company and then on the return, four farms add further interest to a fascinating walk.

The ideal time for this walk is in early spring when the daffodils are at their best. The famous mile and a half path from Low Mill to Church Houses is followed by hundreds of visitors each year. Weekends are obviously the busiest and, therefore, the best time to come is midweek,

or early morning before the crowds arrive. This will also be the time of the best light, especially when it touches petals still damp from overnight rain or morning dew. Unfortunately the daffodils only last for a few weeks, but the walk is still attractive during the rest of the year.

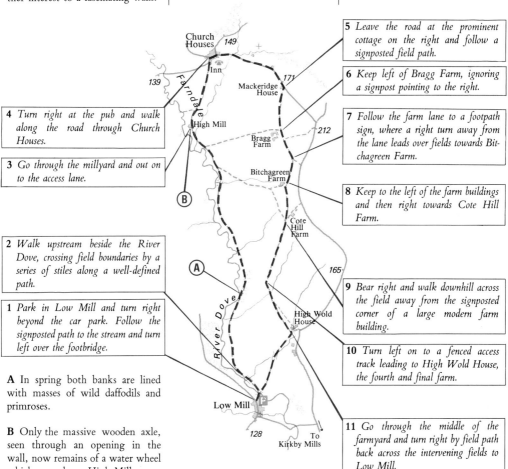

Church Houses 149

Inn

139

Mackeridge House 171

High Mill

Bragg Farm 212

Bitchagreen Farm

B

Cote Hill Farm

A

165

High Wold House

Low Mill

128
To Kirkby Mills

River Dove

Farndale

5 Leave the road at the prominent cottage on the right and follow a signposted field path.

6 Keep left of Bragg Farm, ignoring a signpost pointing to the right.

7 Follow the farm lane to a footpath sign, where a right turn away from the lane leads over fields towards Bitchagreen Farm.

8 Keep to the left of the farm buildings and then right towards Cote Hill Farm.

9 Bear right and walk downhill across the field away from the signposted corner of a large modern farm building.

10 Turn left on to a fenced access track leading to High Wold House, the fourth and final farm.

11 Go through the middle of the farmyard and turn right by field path back across the intervening fields to Low Mill.

4 Turn right at the pub and walk along the road through Church Houses.

3 Go through the millyard and out on to the access lane.

2 Walk upstream beside the River Dove, crossing field boundaries by a series of stiles along a well-defined path.

1 Park in Low Mill and turn right beyond the car park. Follow the signposted path to the stream and turn left over the footbridge.

A In spring both banks are lined with masses of wild daffodils and primroses.

B Only the massive wooden axle, seen through an opening in the wall, now remains of a water wheel which once drove High Mill.

KIRKDALE AND
ST GREGORY'S MINSTER   2½ miles(4 km) Easy/Moderate; 150 feet (46 m)

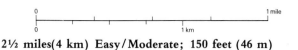

Kirkdale is one of those hidden beauties discovered from time to time. Here is a place to visit on foot rather than by car and as a result, Kirkdale has escaped the over popularisation of easy access.

6 *Turn sharp left at the junction with a narrow track which is followed through an area of low trees as far as the forest edge. Leave the forest at the gate and cross the field in front to follow a pathless route towards a prominent oak tree on the far side. The tree may not be apparent at first, so keep a few degrees to the right of Low Hagg Farm which can be seen ahead on the low ridge.*

5 *Turn sharp right uphill on a forest track.*

4 *A narrow gate leads to a woodland path with the river close by.*

3 *Go through a gate into the field on the left of the track. There is no path, but the route is easy to follow by keeping the forest boundary about 10 yards (9 metres) on the right.*

2 *Go through the gate to the left of the Minster and walk, on a wide path, across an open field by the side of mature beech woodland. Cross Hodge Beck by the small bridge and follow a cart track towards the pine forest.*

1 *The walk starts along the access road to St Gregory's Minster. N.B. Even though there is a car park near the church, respect the wishes of others and park at the road end.*

7 *Go through a narrow gate then downhill along a path confined between wire fences.*

8 *Turn right on a cart track, following it downhill beneath mature pines.*

9 *Left on to a wide gravel surfaced forest track, to climb gently uphill beneath graceful larch trees.*

10 *Where the forest track leaves the wooded area at a white-painted gate, turn sharp right in front of the gate, and walk steeply downhill between the trees, aiming towards the river. Turn left above the river bank opposite St Gregory's Minster and walk on an improving path as far as the Kirkbymoorside road.*

11 *Turn right over the footbridge to reach the end of the walk.*

Low Hagg Farm

114

(B) Hold Caldron

Cat Scar
Thin Oaks Wood

Kirkdale Howl

Hodge Beck

Kirkdale Woods

St. Gregory's Minster

(A)

53 Ford

Kirkdale (Hyena) Caves

(C)

To Kirkbymoorside

A 170

To Helmsley

A St Gregory's Minster. Rebuilt in 1060 by Gorm, a settled Viking — his memorial is the sundial in the porch. Look also for the fine examples of Saxon coffin stones.

B Viewpoint for the middle dale above secluded Hold Caldron.

C Hyena, or Kirkdale, Caves are narrow slits in the quarry wall. It was here in 1921 that the remains of hyena and mammoth bones were found.

Walk 31
UPPER RICCAL DALE
5 miles (8 km) Moderate; 390 feet (191 m)

0   1 mile

0   1 km

The road north from Helmsley to Bransdale must be about the quietest road on the North York Moors. Once it leaves the hamlet of Carlton, the road is the only link with the outside world for a scattering of remote hillfarms and forestry workers' homes.

Away from the car park at the beginning of this walk, the chances of seeing another walker are remote indeed, but you will meet other people along the way, farmers, road workers, foresters, all having their part to play in shaping the countryside. It will be a rare stranger

who cannot spend a few minutes chatting, and the time will be well spent. People who earn their living in remote rural areas are wise in the ways of nature and have a surer grasp on the meaning of life than the most sophisticated city dweller.

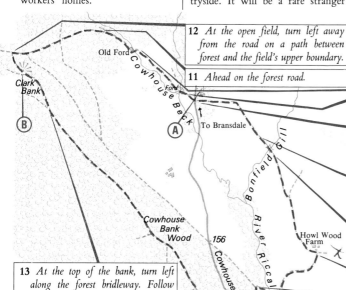

12 At the open field, turn left away from the road on a path between forest and the field's upper boundary.

11 Ahead on the forest road.

10 Follow the garden wall of the farm house, first to the left and then right to join a forest track.

9 Cross the footbridge by the side of the ford. Walk upstream.

8 Cross the metalled road and go through a gate on to a forest road.

7 Go left through the gate at the top of the narrow field beyond the stream to follow the field fence. Bear left across an area of rough grazing and walk towards the road, aiming to the left of the forest chapel whose small tower acts as a landmark.

6 Cross the stream by the footbridge.

5 Go left through the farmyard and left through gate beyond the farm tip to follow a pathless route ahead

4 Go right on the farm road. Cross the footbridge and climb through two fields away from the stream towards Howl Wood Farm. Notice the herculean efforts of previous farmers who built boundary walls from massive boulders cleared from the fields.

13 At the top of the bank, turn left along the forest bridleway. Follow this level track all the way back to Cowhouse Bank car park.

A The tiny chapel tucked beneath boughs of the surrounding pines serves a small community scattered over many miles of moor and forest.

B Clark Bank viewpoint. Bilsdale Moor is to the north. The word 'Bank' is a local term for a steep slope, usually with an access track.

C Viewpoint with a convenient seat!

1 Leave the car in the scenic car park at the top of Cowhouse Bank. Follow the forest track south east over the road into Riccal Dale Wood.

3 Left at the junction with a forest drive.

2 Left at the junction of tracks, walk downhill through the pine forest.

BILSDALE

4¼ miles(7 km) Moderate; 505 feet (154 m)

0   1 mile
0   1 km

Fangdale Beck where this walk starts is, like popular Hutton-le-Hole, a pretty village grouped haphazardly around a stream, but here the similarity ends. Hutton is all ice cream and crowds; Fangdale has none of this, no cafés, no gift shops and only one village store-cum-post office, and overall there is a quiet tranquillity.

Here is the ideal starting point for a pleasant and varied walk. Valley paths wander through riverside meadows and in turn give way to high pasture, reached by an easy climb beneath scented pines.

1 *The walk starts in the village of Fangdale Beck, reached from the B1257. Cross the stream and walk up the path by the side of the church. Turn left on to a farm lane.*

10 *Turn left on regaining the farm lane and return to Fangdale Beck.*

9 *Turn right through a gate in the moorland boundary wall and walk downhill along the intake field. Sheep and cattle are driven this way out to the moor for summer grazing.*

8 *Go left behind the main farm buildings into an old sunken lane. Follow this out through a series of fields towards open moor. On the moor, keep the edge of the forest in sight about 20 yards (18 m) to right.*

7 *Go to the right through the farmyard.*

6 *Turn right along the farm road signposted to Wethercote Farm.*

5 *Fork right and climb by forest track, through a mature pine wood to open fields above.*

2 *Go through the farmyard in front of Malkin Bower Farm, then out along a walled lane.*

3 *At the end of the lane, ignore a prominent path on the left, but turn right to follow a pathless route around the field, joining a more definite path on its upper boundary.*

4 *Pass in front of Helm House Farm and continue by cart track through a series of fields. Where the walled track ends, follow the route by lining up gates as indicated by yellow waymark arrows.*

A The prominent building across the valley, at the side of the Helmsley road, is the Sun Inn. Next to it is restored Spout House, a fine example of an ancient cruck building. This was an earlier Sun Inn and has been carefully restored to preserve its unique form of architecture. The painting of local huntsmen inside the inn was copied, showing them drinking Bovril, which resulted in the company being successfully sued by the artist.

B Viewpoint, south down Bilsdale looking towards Ryedale and the forested slopes of Rievaulx Moor.

C Viewpoint. The mass of Bilsdale East Moor rises up on the far side above Bilsdale and the River Seph.

OSMOTHERLEY

4 miles (6 km) Easy

mixed weather
Snow on Moors.

4/97

```
0                                      1 mile
|——————|——————|——————|——————|——————|
0                        1 km
```

Despite its proximity to industrial Tees-side, Osmotherley manages to retain a picturesque and rural appearance. Built high above the Vale of Mowbray, the lucky positioning of rising ground and semi-natural woodland screen the village from the rumble of traffic along the A19.

There have been people living around Osmotherley since ancient times; the church still retains fragments of Saxon crosses and even older hogsback stones. Carthusian monks settled in a sunny fold beneath the moors for 140 years, until their priory of Mount Grace was plundered on the orders of Henry VIII. The Lady Chapel still stands untouched by the Dissolution; it is the reputed resting place of St Cuthbert.

4 Go left through a narrow gate to follow a path along the upper edge of the wooded escarpment. Pass the strange conglomeration of antennae of the British Telecom station.

5 Walk downhill through woodland and join a wide cart track beyond the woodland gate.

6 On approaching the group of farm buildings, turn left uphill on a field path heading towards the clump of pines sheltering Lady's Chapel. After visiting the chapel, walk ahead on the wide access track.

7 Turn left at the Viewpoint Indicator on to an unsurfaced farm lane.

8 Turn right to return to the village.

1 The walk begins and ends by Osmotherley's ancient market cross and stone market stall, where farm folk used to sell their wares. Walk uphill away from the village.

2 Turn left away from the road at a bridleway signpost along a narrow, unfenced, metalled lane.

3 Where the metalled lane turns sharp left, continue ahead through a gate on a wide, unsurfaced track.

British Telecom & TV Station

Cleveland Way

299

277

242

191

Cod Beck

Dam

Remains of Mount Grace Priory

To A 19

Lady's Chapel

Chapel Wood Farm

Osmotherley

A Down a narrow alley, opposite the market cross, is one of the earliest non-conformist chapels in England —it dates from 1754 and was built shortly after John Wesley preached in the village.

B Traffic along the A19 is glimpsed and occasionally heard far below. Beyond is Cleveland Plain with the Pennines as its western backcloth.

C A partly flagged way leads down from the farm to Mount Grace Priory. The only Carthusian monastery in Yorkshire, it was built between 1397 and 1440. Though a strict order, its monks lived in comparative comfort, each having a two-storied cell with running water from nearby hillside springs, and his own private garden. The Dissolution of 1539 left the beautiful ruins, now owned and preserved by the National Trust.

D Our Lady's Chapel (the 'our' is usually omitted) was built around 1515 as a Chapel of Ease for nearby Mount Grace Priory. St Cuthbert is said to be interred here.

E Viewpoint Indicator, erected by the Osmotherley Civic Society.

HAWNBY HILL

3 miles (5 km) Moderate

0   1 mile

0   1 km

Simplified, this walk is the circuit of Hawnby Hill, but in the three miles it takes to cover the distance, the scenery is a varied composite of everything we can expect to find in this moorland region. Hawnby Hill itself is a narrow whaleback, not quite, but almost, giving itself mountain status. It was left as an outlier of the moors by the Ice Age, whose retreating glacial tongues honed the hill's north-south alignment and gave it its distinctive shape.

Starting in rich farmland, the route climbs out on to the open moor, before dropping to the headwaters of one of the tributaries of the River Rye. Sad ruins of once prosperous farms dot the sides of Ladhill Beck, their lands mostly taken to grow trees foreign to the landscape or used as extra grazing for farms closer to the village.

Hawnby, with its hospitable inn, is one of those places which has little or nothing to offer the tourist who demands gift shops, ice cream parlours and the like, but has much to offer those in search of peace and beauty. It nestles at the southern foot of Hawnby Hill, high above the River Rye. A southward slope away from the village ensures that it gets the maximum sunshine. Sturdy houses built in the warm-coloured local stone complete a charming picture.

6 Cross the stream and turn right away from the lane. Follow a faint path across the heather moor as far as a double stile at the junction of two fields with the moorland boundary. Cross the stiles into the left of the two fields. Walk downhill towards a copse of scrub birch.

5 Cross the moorland road and walk for about 25 yards (23 m) along the gravel lane opposite and into a shallow depression.

4 Go right beyond lonely Hill End House, through a gate on to the open moor following a clear but narrow path.

3 Fork right at the junction of tracks.

2 Turn right at a field gate opposite Manor Farm. Follow a well-defined cart track through a series of fields.

1 The walk starts in the centre of Hawnby. If travelling by car, please take care where it is left as parking is something of a problem in the village. Walk west along the lane past the Hawnby Hotel.

7 Cross the stream at the footbridge. Turn slightly right and walk uphill towards a ruined farm house.

8 Go right in front of the ruins of Crow Nest Farm and descend by an old farm track alongside a field boundary.

9 Go through the gate into a larch plantation on the gradually improving path, with a soft bed of larch needles underfoot.

10 Leave the wood for open fields by the track passing the ruins of Low and Little Banniscue Farms.

11 Turn right at the road. Follow it downhill, over the stream and then climb the short distance back to Hawnby.

A Viewpoint of Upper Ryedale.

B Viewpoint southwards from the village towards Ryedale.

Sportsman's Hall

Moor Gate

207

216

Crow Nest Farm (ruins)

Ladhill Beck

Hawnby Hill Crag

298

Hill End House

294

Hawnby Hill

Low Banniscue Farm (ruins)

Little Banniscue Farm (ruins)

Ladhill Gill

Manor Farm

Hawnby Hotel

127

111

Hawnby

River Rye

Ryedale

Walk 35
HAWNBY CHURCH
4 miles (6 km) Moderate; muddy sections when wet

0   1 mile
0   1 km

Every so often when out walking a church is found which is hidden in some remote corner, well away from the main habitation of its parishioners. Hawnby Church is such: lacking in flamboyant memorials or anything of great architectural merit, nevertheless it has something which many grander places miss: its tranquil atmosphere.

The one word which sums up this walk is — contrast. Starting by the peaceful church, it follows a gentle brook for a short distance before skirting game woods. High farm lands, both arable and grazed, give way to open moorland where the views are of the wildest part of the Hambleton Hills. A dry valley leads back through quiet pasture, disturbed only by the raucous cry of panicking game birds. Finally, a quiet woodland road leads back to Hawnby Church.

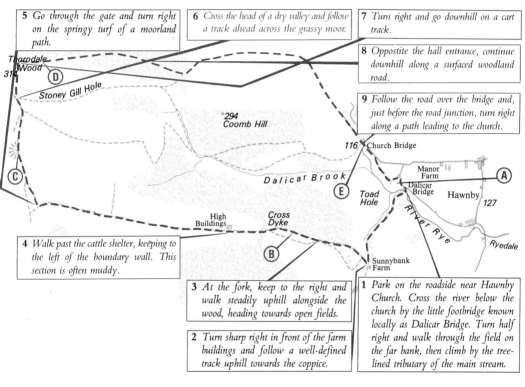

5 Go through the gate and turn right on the springy turf of a moorland path.

6 Cross the head of a dry valley and follow a track ahead across the grassy moor.

7 Turn right and go downhill on a cart track.

8 Opposite the hall entrance, continue downhill along a surfaced woodland road.

9 Follow the road over the bridge and, just before the road junction, turn right along a path leading to the church.

4 Walk past the cattle shelter, keeping to the left of the boundary wall. This section is often muddy.

3 At the fork, keep to the right and walk steadily uphill alongside the wood, heading towards open fields.

2 Turn sharp right in front of the farm buildings and follow a well-defined track uphill towards the coppice.

1 Park on the roadside near Hawnby Church. Cross the river below the church by the little footbridge known locally as Dalicar Bridge. Turn half right and walk through the field on the far bank, then climb by the tree-lined tributary of the main stream.

Thorodale Wood
314
Stoney Gill Hole
294 Coomb Hill
116 Church Bridge
Manor Farm
Dalicar Bridge
Hawnby
127
Toad Hole
Dalicar Brook
River Rye
Ryedale
High Buildings
Cross Dyke
Sunnybank Farm

A The tiny church is well worth a short diversion, especially in early spring when the graveyard is a blaze of yellow from wild daffodils.

B The harsh rattle of pheasants indicates the purpose of the wood as a preserve for rearing game birds.

C Viewpoint. The wild moors of Black Hambleton rise up above Thorodale Woods.

D Viewpoint. The attractive wooded valley is part of the Arden Hall Estate, home of Lord Mexborough.

E Notice the graceful humpbacked design of Church Bridge.

57

Walk 36

KEPWICK AND THE HAMBLETON DROVE ROAD

5 miles (8 km) Strenuous

Black Hambleton, arguably the wildest place on the moors, keeps the bulk of the north easterly storms off Kepwick, and carefully sited belts of maturing trees act as breaks for any of the cruel winds which may creep down off the moors. Kepwick, a quiet secluded backwater where time appears to stand still, enjoys a sunny situation very much the home village to the local manor, in this case Kepwick Hall.

The walk leads quickly away from the pastoral setting of Kepwick to the contrasting harshness of the high moors. Here was the home of Abigail Craister, a witch who lived in a cave on Black Hambleton.

She was said to be able to gets rats and rabbits to work for her.

A wide track follows the western edge of the moors, along the high crest of the Hambleton Hills. This is Hambleton Drove Road, a drove road following a steady course from Cleveland, all the way to Kilburn and the Vale of York.

The system of drove roads is unique and traces of these old routes still survive throughout our remotest regions. Established in medieval times, their use came to its peak during the early part of the Industrial Revolution. Centres of population in Lancashire, Yorkshire, the Black Country and rapidly-expanding London grew at

such a rate that local farmland was unable to cope with the demand for meat. An efficient rail network was still in its infancy and the road system was not designed to cope with the movement of animals. To meet this demand, cattle and sheep were slowly walked south, grazing along the way, to keep them in prime condition. The animals started their trek as far away as the Outer Isles or the Highlands of Scotland and moved south by way of established fairs. In charge of the beasts were a special breed of men, drovers, who thought nothing of living in the open for months on end in order to protect their valuable charges.

A The name, Gallow Hill, at this point speaks of the rough justice given to sheep stealers and highwaymen in less civilised times.

B The view below is of Kepwick Hall, sheltering in the hollow of Eller Beck.

C This is the Hambleton Drove Road, also followed by the Cleveland Way. The broad, mostly unenclosed track allowed cattle and sheep to move freely southwards towards markets in industrial England. Stones set in the heather a little way from the track mark old

land boundaries.

D Drovers were not always popular with local farmers and the walls here were to stop driven animals from eating the grass on the improved and enclosed land on either side.

Over

58

1 *Park where you are sure not to cause inconvenience to others and walk through Kepwick and beyond its church.*

10 *On reaching the road, turn left and follow it back to Kepwick.*

9 *Keep left through the stockyard and then out on to the farm access road. Follow the road past shelter belts of mature trees.*

8 *Cross the stream by a low bridge and go uphill towards Nab Farm.*

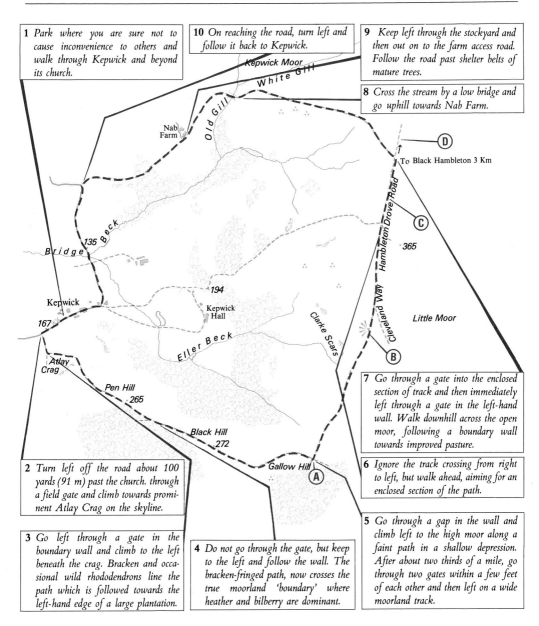

2 *Turn left off the road about 100 yards (91 m) past the church. through a field gate and climb towards prominent Atlay Crag on the skyline.*

3 *Go left through a gate in the boundary wall and climb to the left beneath the crag. Bracken and occasional wild rhododendrons line the path which is followed towards the left-hand edge of a large plantation.*

4 *Do not go through the gate, but keep to the left and follow the wall. The bracken-fringed path, now crosses the true moorland 'boundary' where heather and bilberry are dominant.*

5 *Go through a gap in the wall and climb left to the high moor along a faint path in a shallow depression. After about two thirds of a mile, go through two gates within a few feet of each other and then left on a wide moorland track.*

6 *Ignore the track crossing from right to left, but walk ahead, aiming for an enclosed section of the path.*

7 *Go through a gate into the enclosed section of track and then immediately left through a gate in the left-hand wall. Walk downhill across the open moor, following a boundary wall towards improved pasture.*

St Aeldred, third Abbot of Rievaulx, thought of the abbey as a place of peace and serenity and somewhere to escape from the tumult of the world, and if he came back today he would still echo those thoughts. Tucked away in a fold between wooded hills where Ryedale is joined by Nettle Dale, the soaring arches of the ruined windows stand out in majesty amid peaceful surroundings.

Cistercian monks built an abbey here in 1132 and over the years, until 1538, they amassed tremendous wealth from their many lucrative interests. Owning vast areas of land,

they were shrewd enough to exploit whatever natural riches came with them. Ironstone, mined on the nearby moors, was smelted into metal for the rapidly expanding economy. Sheep walks covered many miles of moors and salt, produced near the sea, was sold to preserve fish caught by fishermen obliged to give tithes to the abbey.

Above the abbey is Rievaulx Terrace, an 18th century pleasure garden laid out in the fashionable style of the time by Thomas Dunscombe. At the northern end of the terrace, a mock Ionic Temple gazes down from its pillared portico

above the ruined abbey. A Tuscan Temple to the south complements the idyllic scene. Owned by the National Trust, the grounds are a riot of wild woodland flowers in spring and summer.

The walk described below is short, but full of interest. The size of the abbey can be appreciated from the number of mounds and walls dotting the fields around, as well as the central ruins. Easy strolling through a meadow leads on to flowery woodland where the soft sound of wood pigeons sets the scene for views of abbey and terrace.

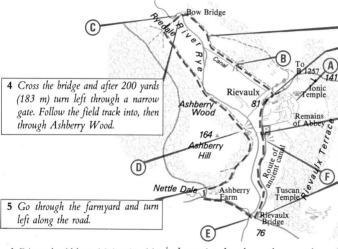

3 Climb up to and over a stile, then turn left into the lane.

2 Turn left away from the road along the path signposted to Bow Bridge.

4 Cross the bridge and after 200 yards (183 m) turn left through a narrow gate. Follow the field track into, then through Ashberry Wood.

1 The walk is from Rievaulx Abbey and starts by the car park. Turn right and walk along the road towards the village.

6 Go left at the road junction and along riverside lane back to the abbey.

5 Go through the farmyard and turn left along the road.

A Rievaulx Abbey. Maintained by English Heritage. Information, guide books and light refreshments are available at the entrance kiosk.

B A backward view of the abbey also shows the attractive houses of Rievaulx village. The water-filled

depression by the path once channelled the abbey water supply.

C Bow Bridge, a hump-backed pack-horse bridge.

D Leafy boughs frame the romantic ruins of the abbey.   Above, the

scene is completed by the Ionic Temple on Rievaulx Terrace.

E Look over the bridge at the attractive woodland setting of the River Rye.

F Fine roadside view of the abbey.

SUTTON BANK

2½ miles (4 km) Easy; one uphill section 430 feet (131 m)

The sharp western escarpment of the Hambleton Hills is the setting for this short walk, which is full of interest from start to finish. Alkaline sandstone rocks, which make up the visible upper reaches of Sutton Brow and Whitestone Cliff, were laid down in a tropical sea millions of years ago. Later flooding following the Ice Age, and the ice itself, carved the steep hillside, but also left the distinctly-shaped lower hills outlying between the escarpment and the Vale of Mowbray. The warm hues of this soft sandstone were favoured until recently,

in the industrial north, where it was known as donkey stone and used for scouring and edging doorsteps.

Lake Gormire is a unique feature in a region normally lacking in natural standing water. It was formed about 20,000 years ago when a glacial landslide blocked the hollow between the escarpment and Gormire Rigg. The lake appears to regulate itself by underground drainage. Beech, sycamore and ash woodland surround the lake, but on the moor edge growth tends to be mostly scrubby hawthorn with wild

pine, birch and mountain ash established in sheltered pockets. Flowers also have their own well-defined zones; heather grows in places exposed to the strong prevailing winds, and rock rose on sunny outcrops, while woodland flowers like bluebells will only grow on damp ground where water seeps between the alkaline sandstone and underlying shales.

An easily-read guide describes the Nature Trail which follows part of this walk. Features on the trail are marked by numbered guide posts.

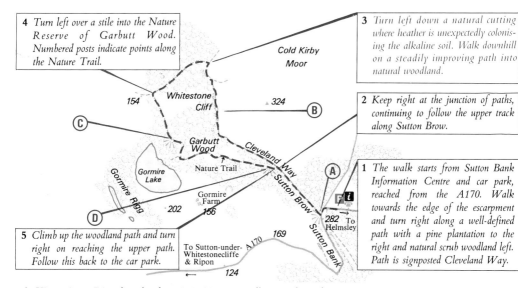

4 *Turn left over a stile into the Nature Reserve of Garbutt Wood. Numbered posts indicate points along the Nature Trail.*

3 *Turn left down a natural cutting where heather is unexpectedly colonising the alkaline soil. Walk downhill on a steadily improving path into natural woodland.*

2 *Keep right at the junction of paths, continuing to follow the upper track along Sutton Brow.*

1 *The walk starts from Sutton Bank Information Centre and car park, reached from the A170. Walk towards the edge of the escarpment and turn right along a well-defined path with a pine plantation to the right and natural scrub woodland left. Path is signposted Cleveland Way.*

5 *Climb up the woodland path and turn right on reaching the upper path. Follow this back to the car park.*

A Viewpoint. Directly ahead is Sutton - under - Whitestonecliffe village, beyond stretches the Vale of Mowbray with the Vale of York to the south. Further west, the Pennines range on either side of the broad mouth of Wensleydale.

B Training gallops to the right are linked with an old racecourse which used the flat lands of Cold Kirby Moor. Races started from Dialstone Farm, to the east, so called from a weighing-in scale in its wall.

C Viewpoint. Gormire Lake, the largest natural standing water on the North York Moors, can be glimpsed through trees. Unofficial side paths lead down to the lakeside.

D Viewpoint.

BYLAND ABBEY
3¾ miles(6 km) Moderate

One of the functions of medieval abbeys was that of education, a tradition which continues to this day at Ampleforth Abbey and College. This modern ecclesiastical seat of learning can be seen in the distance, a little way beyond the contrasting ruins of Byland Abbey.

Cisterian monks came to this country from France in 1123 and founded Furness Abbey in the Lake District. Moving their abbey seven times in forty-three years, they eventually came to North Yorkshire and established Byland Abbey in 1177, after trying several sites in the area, building Byland on what had once been a swamp.

The extensive drainage works, which had to be carried out in order to make the site more habitable, can be appreciated by channels which now flow through the first-rate agricultural land to the south of this walk. It took something in the order of sixty years to complete these improvements, but in the end the abbey had its own drinking water and sanitation, also a mill pond together with a series of fish ponds. Market gardens provided fresh vegetables and made the abbey completely self supporting.

Byland Abbey is cared for by English Heritage.

Newburgh Priory, which housed twenty-six canons from 1150 to 1539, is not far away, as is also Shandy Hall at Coxwold, the 18th-century home of humorist Laurence Sterne. It was here, whilst he was a vicar of Coxwold, that he wrote his novels *Sentimental Journey, Journal to Eliza,* and *Tristram Shandy.* The Hall is now a museum, devoted mainly to Sterne and his life in the mellow atmosphere of the tranquil village of Coxwold.

A Good views of Byland Abbey.

B Even though the 'free view' of the abbey from the perimeter fence gives a clear indication of its layout, it is better to make a diversion and explore the serene ruins at close quarters.

The remains of this once-extensive abbey, built under the leadership of Abbot Roger, are only a fraction of the buildings which covered the site until the Dissolution. Abbot Roger is said to have chosen this damp site as an alternative to Old Byland, as a means of escaping the competing sound of nearby Rievaulx's bells. Old Byland, abandoned as an abbey, became a grange farm providing meat and wool for the monks.

From the roadside the first building which catches the eye is the almost-intact gatehouse, but by far the most imposing part of the ruins is the south transept, a lasting memorial to the 12th century monks who worshipped here. A small museum holds relics unearthed from the ecclesiastical past and helps to explain the complexities of Byland Abbey as it once was.

C Ampleforth Abbey and its College are outlined on the eastern horizon.

Over

0   1 mile

0   1 km

1 *The walk starts in Wass village. Parking is limited, so please make sure that you are not blocking someone's access. Walk uphill away from the cross roads along the minor lane leading towards Abbey Bank Wood.*

2 *Turn left through the gate beyond the last house on the left and walk across fields with the woods on your right.*

11 *A stile marks the crossing point of the stream. Continue and rejoin the road about 120 yards (110 m), before it turns sharp right. Turn right and so back to Wass.*

10 *Follow the fence to the right, towards woodland, and cross the fence by a stile. Keep to the left of Carr House as far as its access drive. Cross the latter by two stiles and walk downhill over the field, aiming towards the lower part of a narrow belt of trees marking the course of a small stream.*

9 *Cross the stile into the field on the right and climb the rising ground in front. There is no established path across this field, but aim uphill and slightly to the right until a wire fence is reached.*

8 *Turn left downhill along the road for about 100 yards (91 m).*

3 *Keep to the left of Abbey House Farm. Walk down the drive and cross the main road. Go through a gate to the left of the abbey and follow a field path around the perimeter fence.*

4 *Follow the field boundary to the left away from the abbey, then go downhill into a shallow hollow, crossing fields in the direction of Low Pasture House Farm which will be seen ahead.*

5 *Keep to the left of the farm and up to a ruined barn. Follow the boundary fence beyond the barn, downhill towards a small wooded hill. Cross the fence at a stile and over two fields to Wass Grange Farm.*

6 *Do not go into the farmyard but turn right and walk along the field track alongside a boundary fence. Keep to the left of a fenced area of scrub and young trees which is used for rearing game birds. Cross the shallow valley and then the stream by a narrow footbridge. Climb through scrubby wood towards a grassy ridge.*

7 *Walk uphill to the right of a group of wooden holiday chalets and join the main road.*

Walk 40
KILBURN WHITE HORSE
3 miles (5km) Easy

Kilburn White Horse was dug by children from Kilburn school in 1857 under the direction of their schoolmaster, John Hodgson, and its designer, Thomas Taylor. 314 feet (96 m) long and 228 feet (70 m) high, the structure is regularly maintained by the Kilburn White Horse Association.

As a walk, with or without the White Horse, there is something for everyone. A level path wanders along the escarpment, then descends into the forest before climbing back up Roulston Scar. The views are superlative, ranging from the Yorkshire Wolds to the Pennines far away across the Vale of Mowbray; York and its Minster can often be seen to the south.

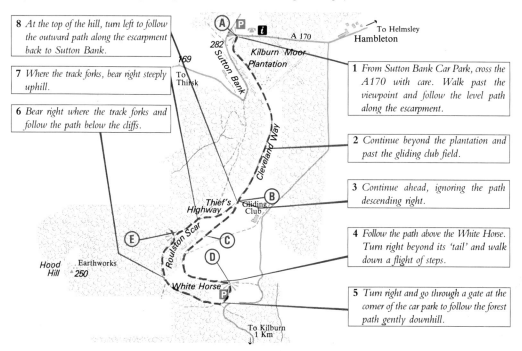

8 At the top of the hill, turn left to follow the outward path along the escarpment back to Sutton Bank.

7 Where the track forks, bear right steeply uphill.

6 Bear right where the track forks and follow the path below the cliffs.

1 From Sutton Bank Car Park, cross the A170 with care. Walk past the viewpoint and follow the level path along the escarpment.

2 Continue beyond the plantation and past the gliding club field.

3 Continue ahead, ignoring the path descending right.

4 Follow the path above the White Horse. Turn right beyond its 'tail' and walk down a flight of steps.

5 Turn right and go through a gate at the corner of the car park to follow the forest path gently downhill.

A Viewpoint. The Vale of York is below with the Pennines as its backcloth.

B The narrow path on the right which you will ascend later is known as the 'Thief's Highway', once the escape route of a notorious highwayman who plundered travellers on nearby Hambleton

Drove Road. The drove was used by cattle on their way south from Scotland.

C The path follows the western boundary of The Yorkshire Gliding Club's airfield. Look out for low flying aircraft and falling towlines.

D Viewpoint. The White Horse is below. Please do not walk on it, but keep to the path and prevent erosion. Beyond, across the Vale of Pickering, are the Wolds and on a clear day you may see York Minster 18 miles (29 km) away.

E Viewpoint. Iron Age earthworks line the summit of Hood Hill.